The Balance
of the NIV

The Balance of the NIV

of the NIV

What Makes a Good Translation

Kenneth L. Barker

Baker Books

A Division of Baker Book House Co
Grand Rapids, Michigan 49516

©1999 by Kenneth L. Barker

Published by Baker Books
a division of Baker Book House Company
P.O. Box 6287, Grand Rapids, MI 49516–6287

Printed in the United States of America

Unless otherwise indicated Scripture quotations are taken from the HOLY
BIBLE, NEW INTERNATIONAL VERSION® NIV®. Copyright © 1973, 1978,

Library of Congress Cataloging-in-Publication Data

Barker, Kenneth L.
    The balance of the NIV: what makes a good translation / Ken-
neth L. Barker.
        p.   cm.
    Includes bibliographical references and indexes.
    ISBN 0–8010-6239-X (pbk.)
    1. Bible.—English—Versions—New International—History.
I. Title.
BS195.N372 B373 2000
220.5′20818—dc21   99-052526

1984 by International Bible Society. Used by permission of Zondervan Pub-
lishing House. All rights reserved.

For information about academic books, resources for Christian leaders, and
all new releases from Baker Book House, visit our website:
                    http://www.bakerbooks.com

To the millions
of past, present, and future
readers and users of the NIV
and to all my students and teachers
from whom I have learned so much
through the years—
and for the glory of God
and the advancement of his Word
in all the earth

Contents

Abbreviations

All abbreviations used in this book are listed and explained below, except the books of the Bible. For these I have used quite standard abbreviations, which should be familiar to most, if not all, readers. The bibliography provides complete information on the works referred to here.

AB	Anchor Bible
Assn.	Association
ASV	American Standard Version
AV	Authorized Version (KJV)
BA	*Biblical Archaeologist*
BASOR	*Bulletin of the American Schools of Oriental Research*
BDB	F. Brown, S.R. Driver, and C.A. Briggs, *A Hebrew and English Lexicon of the Old Testament*
Bib	*Biblica*
Bib. Sac.	*Bibliotheca Sacra*
BR	*Bible Review*
c.	about
CBT	Committee on Bible Translation (NIV)
CE	Common Era (= A.D.)
CEV	Contemporary English Version
cf.	compare
CRC	Christian Reformed Church
CT	*Christianity Today*

EBC	*Expositor's Bible Commentary* (F.E. Gaebelein, ed.)
ed(s).	editor(s); edition(s)
e.g.	for example
ETA	Evangelical Training Association
et al.	and others
etc.	and so forth
ETS	Evangelical Theological Society
gen.	general
GKC	*Gesenius' Hebrew Grammar,* ed. E. Kautzsch, trans. A.E. Cowley
GNB	Good News Bible (TEV)
GTJ	*Grace Theological Journal*
HALOT	*Hebrew and Aramaic Lexicon of the Old Testament* (Koehler and Baumgartner; trans. M.E.J. Richardson)
Ibid.	same
IBS	International Bible Society
i.e.	that is
JB	Jerusalem Bible
JBL	*Journal of Biblical Literature*
JETS	*Journal of the Evangelical Theological Society*
KJV	King James Version (AV)
lit.	literally
LXX	Septuagint (Greek translation of Old Testament)
MS(S)	manuscript(s)
MT	Masoretic Text (traditional Hebrew text)
n.	note
NAB	New American Bible
NAC	New American Commentary
NAE	National Assn. of Evangelicals
NASB	New American Standard Bible (1995 update)
NCBC	New Century Bible Commentary

NCV	New Century Version
n.d.	no date given
NEB	New English Bible
NICNT	New International Commentary on the New Testament
NICOT	New International Commentary on the Old Testament
NIDOTTE	*New International Dictionary of Old Testament Theology and Exegesis* (W.A. VanGemeren, ed.)
NIrV	New International Reader's Version
NIV	New International Version
NIVSB	*The NIV Study Bible* (K.L. Barker, ed.)
NJB	New Jerusalem Bible
NKJV	New King James Version
NLT	New Living Translation
NRSV	New Revised Standard Version
OTL	Old Testament Library
p(p).	page(s)
REB	Revised English Bible
repr.	reprint
rev.	revised
RR	*Reformed Review*
RSV	Revised Standard Version
RV	Revised Version
SD	Studies and Documents
TDOT	*Theological Dictionary of the Old Testament* (G.J. Botterweck and H. Ringgren, eds.)
TEV	Today's English Version (GNB)
TJ	*Trinity Journal*
TOTC	Tyndale Old Testament Commentaries
TR	Textus Receptus ("received text")
trans.	translator
Ugar.	Ugaritic
v(v).	verse(s)

WBC	Word Biblical Commentary
WEC	Wycliffe Exegetical Commentary
WTJ	*Westminster Theological Journal*
ZPEB	*Zondervan Pictorial Encyclopedia of the Bible* (M.C. Tenney, ed.)

1

Balance Is the Key

If the church is to hear God's Word with authority, accuracy, and clarity, it must use a good translation. But that raises the question: What constitutes a good translation? In the opinion of many, the key word is *balance*. A good translation will exhibit a pleasing balance in at least five areas.

First, a good translation will take a balanced committee approach. The New International Version of the Bible (NIV) is governed by the fifteen-person Committee on Bible Translation (CBT). (It has been my privilege to serve as secretary of CBT since 1975.) CBT has always had broad representation denominationally and theologically within evangelicalism. Its current members are Kenneth L. Barker, retired from International Bible Society as executive director of their NIV Translation Center; Gordon D. Fee, Regent College (Vancouver); Richard T. France, retired from Wycliffe Hall, Oxford, and from pastoral ministry in the Church of England; R. Laird Harris, retired from Covenant Theological Seminary; Karen H. Jobes, Westmont College; Walter L. Liefeld, retired from Trinity Evangelical Divinity School; Donald H. Madvig, retired from pastoring an Evangelical Covenant Church; Douglas J. Moo, Trinity Evangelical Divinity School; Martin J. Selman, Spurgeon's College (London); John H. Stek, retired from Calvin Theological Seminary; Larry Walker, retired from Mid-America Baptist Theological Seminary; Bruce K. Waltke, Regent

College (Vancouver) and Reformed Theological Seminary (Orlando); Herbert M. Wolf, Wheaton College Graduate School; and Ronald F. Youngblood, Bethel Theological Seminary (West Campus). (The fact that only fourteen names are listed here indicates that one vacancy presently exists on CBT.)

Such a balanced, broad representation has resulted in wide acceptance of the NIV within Christianity as a whole. In fact, the following denominations and other religious bodies either officially sanction or extensively use the NIV:

American Baptist
Assemblies of God
Baptist General Conference
Christian & Missionary Alliance
Christian Reformed
Church of Christ
Church of God
Church of Ireland
Church of the Nazarene
Conservative Baptist
Episcopal
Evangelical Covenant
Evangelical Free
Free Methodist
Grace Brethren
General Assn. of Regular Baptist
Independent (Bible)
Mennonite
Methodist
Missouri Lutheran Synod
Plymouth Brethren

Presbyterian
Reformed Baptist
Reformed Church of America
Reformed Episcopal
Seventh Day Adventist
Southern Baptist
United Brethren
Wisconsin Lutheran Synod

The Canadian Reformed Churches are the most recent addition to this list.

Second, a good translation will have a balanced textual basis. For example, a balanced translation like the NIV will not follow any single group, family, or type of Greek manuscripts of the New Testament 100 percent of the time (see chapter 3 for details).

Third, a good translation will follow a balanced translation philosophy. This means that it will be neither too literal nor too free; rather, it will take a mediating approach to the translation task. Such a balanced method is probably the primary reason for the NIV's phenomenal success (other than God's sovereignty and providence). Since 1986 the NIV has been the best-selling English version of the Bible. Slightly over one out of every three new Bibles sold today is an NIV. There are well over 120 million copies of NIV Bibles and New Testaments in print. Apparently, millions of people were searching for the most balanced version among all the available Bibles, and they believe they have found it in the NIV. It took the KJV almost 400 years to pass the 300 million mark in sales and distribution. If the current trend continues, the NIV will have surpassed that record in approximately 50 years (counting from 1978).[1]

Fourth, a good translation will use balance in handling difficult passages (see chapter 5 for details).

Fifth, a good translation will have a wide range of balanced works available to support its text (see chapter 6 for details).

These five essential areas of balance will now be developed more fully. However, since this introductory chapter has made no reference to several other questions that are frequently asked about the NIV, the reader's attention is first directed to the appendix, where some of these other questions are dealt with. It should also be noted here that this book is, in some respects, an expansion of a summary chapter that only recently appeared in print.[2]

2

A Balanced
Committee Approach

In tracing the history of the NIV, one discovers that in 1965 a joint Bible translation committee of the Christian Reformed Church and the National Association of Evangelicals appointed a fifteen-person Committee on Bible Translation (CBT) to oversee the "preparation of a contemporary English translation of the Bible . . . as a collegiate endeavor of evangelical scholars."[1] CBT was to have broad representation denominationally and theologically within evangelicalism. Yet the aim was not to produce an "evangelical" translation but one that would accurately and clearly communicate what the Bible actually says and means. The translators were to be fully committed to the inspiration, infallibility, and divine authority of Holy Scripture as nothing less than the very Word of God.

In fact, CBT's Constitution requires that all NIV translators subscribe to the doctrinal statement of the Evangelical Theological Society (ETS) or to the statement on Scripture in the Westminster Confession, Belgic Confession, New Hampshire Confession, or the creedal basis of the National Association of Evangelicals (NAE) or some other comparable statement. The ETS statement reads: "The Bible alone, and the Bible in its entirety, is the Word of God written and is therefore inerrant in the autographs. God is a Trinity, Father, Son, and Holy Spirit, each an uncreated person, one in essence, equal in power and glory."

As far as the other confessions of faith mentioned above are concerned, it is well known that the Reformation creeds clearly speak of the complete truthfulness and trustworthiness of the Bible. The Westminster Confession speaks of the Bible's "infallible truth" and of believing "to be true whatsoever is revealed in the Word." The Belgic Confession affirms, "We reject with all our hearts whatsoever doth not agree with this infallible rule." The New Hampshire Confession declares that "the Holy Bible was written by men divinely inspired . . . it has God for its author, salvation for its end, and truth without any admixture of error for its matter." The NAE statement says, "We believe the Bible to be the inspired, the only infallible, authoritative Word of God."

What was the actual process or working method of the NIV translators? It may be diagrammed like this:

The pyramid shape indicates that as one moves upward from the bottom, the number of translation scholars decreases until only fifteen (CBT) are involved at the top. One of the distinguishing features of the NIV was an exhaustive review process for each book of the Bible. To explain:

First, Initial Translation Teams (involving almost 125 scholars from the major English-speaking countries of the world) translated the biblical books from the Hebrew and Aramaic texts of the Old Testament and from the Greek of the New Testament. CBT assigned each book of the Bible to a team of three to five scholars, chosen on the basis of their ability and interest; all of them possessed recognized expertise in the books they worked on. Their basic, fresh translations were given to one of several Intermediate Editorial Committees.

Second, Intermediate Editorial Committees reviewed and evaluated the initial translations and compiled suggestions for improvement. These committees were comprised of five to seven translators. They checked the work carefully against the Hebrew, Aramaic, and Greek texts and also began the process of improving English style. Since these committees changed from session to session, their variety gave freshness to the translation.

Third, General Editorial Committees evaluated the work of the two previous committee levels and made new suggestions. They were also comprised of five to seven members. Once again they carefully checked the original languages for accuracy of rendering and further improved the style.

Fourth, CBT reviewed and evaluated all previous work and determined the final content and wording of the NIV. We accomplished that by reference to the original-language texts, by paying attention to unity and continuity, and by making additional improvements in English style.

Fifth, English stylists and critics improved the literary quality of the NIV. The two primary stylists (Frank Gaebelein and Margaret Nicholson) read each word of every book twice and made numerous valuable suggestions for change.

Sixth, the NIV was field-tested. As samples of the NIV were completed, they were distributed to pastors and church members—highly educated and less well educated, young and old—in order to solicit suggestions to improve clarity.

Seventh, CBT put the NIV in final form.

What are the strengths and advantages of such a balanced and thorough approach to the task of translating the Bible? They include these:

1. No one person can spot all the problems in a translation. All translators have areas of weakness as well as of strength. A team of translators, however, can nicely supplement and complement one another.

2. Linguistic studies are highly specialized today. No one person can be an expert in all the diverse fields, such as Hebrew, Aramaic, Ugaritic, Akkadian, Greek Septuagint, Latin Vulgate, Syriac Peshitta, New Testament Greek, textual criticism, the science of general linguistics, and English style. A committee of scholars can provide specialists in all the above areas and, if necessary, use the services of consultants.

3. Ecclesiastical, theological, and linguistic provincialisms are avoided.

4. When a translation problem arises, the committee approach is conducive to finding a solution. Vigorous discussion and cross-fertilization of ideas act as a catalyst to stimulate the mind, thereby producing solutions that would never have been reached by a single individual working independently.

5. The multitiered process yields a finely honed product. At the lower editorial levels attention can be given to major problems. Once these have been solved, it becomes possible to concentrate on finer points and "polish" the final product.

6. As indicated in chapter 1, the committee approach results in wider acceptance of the version within Christianity.

If a college faculty is, at least in part, a community of scholars dedicated to seeking the truth, the NIV translators were a community of Christian scholars dedicated to the clear and faithful rendering of God's Truth into contemporary, idiomatic English. Their association became a true biblical *koinōnia*—a vital "fellowship" in Christ the Lord. Out of this came deepening insight into the demands of faithful translation and a surer feeling for the nuances of NIV style.

Such a collegial setting is also conducive to experiencing certain personal benefits. For me, it was first of all an experience in *fellowship* with some of God's greatest servants. Second, it was an experience in *humility*. It was humbling to be voted down after lengthy argumentation. In fact, based on my experience as a Bible translator (NIV, NIrV, NASB), I have often said, "If you want to discover how little you really know, become involved in translating all the books of the Bible from Hebrew, Aramaic, and Greek into English or any other language." I concur with Martin Luther, who said, "It is good for me that I have been involved in translating the Bible, for otherwise I might have died with the fond persuasion that I am learned."[2]

Third, it was a *broadening* experience. I gained a greater appreciation for the *whole* Body of Christ instead of just one small segment of it. Fourth, it was an experience in *sovereignty*. I had to learn to trust that the sovereign God, through his Spirit and in answer to prayer, was somehow accomplishing his will in the final decisions of the majority of CBT whether I always fully agreed with those decisions personally or not. For these experiences I am humbly grateful to the Lord.

So a good translation will take a balanced committee approach.

3

A Balanced Textual Basis

The Old Testament

What was the textual basis of the NIV Old Testament? The question is answered in a general way in the preface to the NIV:

> For the Old Testament the standard Hebrew [and Aramaic] text, the Masoretic Text as published in the latest editions of *Biblia Hebraica,* was used throughout. The Dead Sea Scrolls contain material bearing on an earlier stage of the Hebrew text. They were consulted, as were the Samaritan Pentateuch and the ancient scribal traditions relating to textual changes. Sometimes a variant Hebrew reading in the margin of the Masoretic Text was followed instead of the text itself. Such instances, being variants within the Masoretic tradition, are not specified by footnotes. In rare cases, words in the consonantal text were divided differently from the way they appear in the Masoretic Text. Footnotes indicate this. The translators also consulted the more important early versions—the Septuagint; Symmachus and Theodotion; the Vulgate; the Syriac Peshitta; the Targums; and for the Psalms the *Juxta Hebraica* of Jerome. Readings from these versions were occasionally followed where the Masoretic Text seemed doubtful and where accepted principles of textual criticism showed that one or more of these textual witnesses appeared to provide the correct reading. Such instances are footnoted. Sometimes vowel letters and vowel signs did not, in the judgment

of the translators, represent the correct vowels for the original consonantal text. Accordingly some words were read with a different set of vowels. These instances are usually not indicated by footnotes.

Clearly, priority was given to the Masoretic Text (MT, the traditional Hebrew text)—and correctly so. Childs's thesis is that "the Masoretic text of the Hebrew Bible is the *vehicle* both for recovering and for understanding the canonical text of the Old Testament."[1] Barrera agrees:

> Ultimately, the MT is a text which has been transmitted with the utmost care in every period of its history, even from the period before the consonantal text was fixed in the second century CE. The MT is therefore the starting point and obligatory reference for all work on OT text criticism. . . . However, the MT is neither the only nor always the best text.[2]

Metzger elaborates on what is meant by "utmost care":

> How did it come about that Hebrew manuscripts were transmitted with such a relatively high degree of accuracy? The primary answer is that the guild of Jewish scribes took extraordinary care in its work. Furthermore scribes had developed rules which ensured as high a degree of accuracy as possible in transmitting the manuscripts of the Old Testament. The Masoretes collected statistics on the number of words in each book of the Hebrew scriptures. They could identify the middle word in each biblical book. When encountering in the text the sacred name of Yahweh, the scribe would rise, go to a basin of water, and ceremonially wash his hands before returning to transcribe this holy name. That kind of care enables us to understand the high degree of accuracy that was attained in the transmission of Old Testament manuscripts.[3]

Similarly, Tov declares, "On the whole, the readings of the MT do deserve more respect than readings found in other sources."[4] In my opinion, several other modern English versions of the Bible are not as faithful to the MT as they should be. Too many translation scholars have felt free to have a field day in conjecturally emending verse after verse on nearly every page. Surely such unbridled freedom must be more restricted by adherence to generally accepted canons or principles of textual criticism. I, for one, have been gratified and encouraged by the recent trend toward greater respect for the MT.

When it comes to formulating and applying principles of textual criticism, probably most of the NIV translators would concur with Waltke:

> In the light of [the] varied history [of the text of the Hebrew Bible], it is not surprising that a strictly prescribed method of OT textual criticism has never been worked out. There are, however, basic rules that help place the criticism of the OT text on firm basis in order to avoid arbitrariness and subjectivity.
>
> 1. Where the Hebrew MSS and ancient versions agree, it may be assumed that the original reading has been preserved.
>
> 2. Where Hebrew MSS and ancient versions differ among themselves, one should choose either the more difficult reading . . . from the point of view of language and subject matter or the reading that most readily makes the development of the other reading(s) intelligible. To make this choice, one should be fully knowledgeable of the history and character of the recensions. . . . Moreover, these criteria should be understood as complementing one another so that one may arrive at a reasonable and worthy text, for a "more difficult reading" does not mean a "meaningless and corrupt reading."
>
> 3. Where Hebrew MSS and ancient versions offer good and sensible readings and a superior reading cannot be

demonstrated on the basis of the above two rules, one should, as a matter of first principle, allow MT to stand.

4. Where Hebrew MSS and ancient versions differ and none offers a passable sense, one may attempt a conjecture concerning the true reading—a conjecture that must be validated by demonstrating the process of the textual corruption from the original to the existing text-forms. Such conjectures, however, can never be used to validate the interpretation of the whole passage in that they will have been made on the basis of an expectation derived from the whole.[5]

Three examples will show some "accepted principles of textual criticism" in operation. All of them are selected from my commentary on Zechariah.[6] The first principle pertains to passages where the Hebrew MSS and the ancient versions all agree on the reading, and this single reading yields a good sense. In such passages it may be safely assumed that the original reading has been preserved. In Zechariah 6:11, for example, the Lord instructs the prophet: "Take the silver and gold and make a crown, and set it on the head of the high priest, Joshua son of Jehozadak." Some interpreters argue that the original reading at the end of the verse was "Zerubbabel son of Shealtiel" instead of "Joshua son of Jehozadak." But Eichrodt rightly considers "that the interpretation of this passage in terms of Zerubbabel, which can only be secured at the cost of hazardous conjecture, is mistaken, and that a reference to a hoped-for messianic ruler after Zerubbabel's disappearance is more in accordance with the evidence."[7] Furthermore, no Hebrew MSS or ancient versions have the Zerubbabel reading. Therefore, because it is a purely conjectural emendation, we reject it.

The second principle applies to passages where the Hebrew MSS and the ancient versions differ among themselves. In that situation one should choose either the more difficult reading or the reading that most readily explains how the others arose. It is also important to remember that a more difficult reading does not mean a meaningless and obviously corrupt reading, for the end result must be a reasonable and worthy text. Zechariah 5:6, for instance, interprets the ephah or measuring basket (or barrel) as "the iniquity of the people throughout the land," in harmony with verse 8. But the Hebrew word *ʿênām* presents a textual problem. As it stands, it means "their eye" (i.e., their appearance), which does not yield a good sense (cf. the parallel in v. 8, where the woman in the basket is interpreted as wickedness personified). The NIV, probably correctly, follows one Hebrew MS, the Septuagint, and the Syriac in reading *ʿǎwōnām* ("their iniquity"). (The pronoun "their" refers to the people, perhaps with special reference to the godless rich.) The only significant variation between the two readings is the Hebrew letter *waw (w)* instead of *yodh (y)*. Even here it should be borne in mind that in many ancient Hebrew MSS the only perceptible difference between the two letters is the length of the downward stroke. A long *yodh* and a short *waw* are virtually indistinguishable, so it would be easy for a scribe to miscopy. To further support the reading, "their iniquity (or perversity)," Baldwin adds:

> The ephah, named by Amos in his invective on short measure given by the merchants (Am. 8:5), symbolized injustice in *all the land*. The life of the community was vitiated by iniquity that infected it in every part (cf. Hg. 2:14). The meanness that prompted the making of false measures was a symptom of an underlying perversity that was at the root of perverse actions and relationships.[8]

The third textual principle relates to passages where both the Hebrew MSS and the ancient versions offer good and sensible readings, and a superior reading cannot be demonstrated on the basis of the above two principles. In that case, one should give priority to the MT. An example of such a passage appears to be Zechariah 14:5, which reads: "You will flee by my mountain valley, for it will extend to Azel. You will flee as you fled from the earthquake in the days of Uzziah king of Judah." The NIV footnote offers this alternative translation: "My mountain valley will be blocked and will extend to Azel. It will be blocked as it was blocked because of the earthquake in the days of Uzziah king of Judah." This alternative rendering presupposes revocalizing the verbs to *nistam* (from *stm*) and receives support from the Septuagint, the Aramaic Targum, and Symmachus (Greek). The MT, on the other hand, has *nastem* (from *nws*) and is supported by the Latin Vulgate and the Syriac Peshitta. As I perceive it, the meaning of this reading (the MT) is that the newly created east–west valley (Zech. 14:4) will afford an easy means of rapid escape from the anti-Semitic onslaught detailed in verse 2. (The Mount of Olives has always constituted a serious obstacle to such an escape to the east.) Since the MT makes good sense and there is no convincing reason to change it, it is to be preferred.

If readers also desire an illustration of Waltke's fourth textual rule above, they may find one in Proverbs 26:23. It will be recalled that the fourth principle has to do with those rare instances where none of the existing texts presents a passable sense. In such a situation, one may attempt a conjecture concerning the true reading—a conjecture that must be validated by demonstrating the process of the textual corruption from the original to the existing text-forms. In the process of Old Testament text transmission, even the most careful scribe occasionally committed an error in judgment. One type of such an error is fission, the division of a single word into two.

Apparently this error was made in Proverbs 26:23. The scribal mistake was discovered by Ginsberg[9] and was acknowledged by Albright.[10] Perhaps the mistake was made because it involves a rare poetic word that was not in common use and so eventually dropped from the language. Whatever the reason, in the proverb a person with fervent (or smooth) lips but a wicked heart is compared, as the MT now stands, to an earthen vessel overlaid with "silver dross" or "dross silver." The text is difficult for at least two reasons. First, the Hebrew expression means literally "silver of dross," on which Albright aptly comments parenthetically, "(whatever that might mean)."[11] Second, silver dross, or dross silver, was not used in plating earthenware, nor would it make an attractive exterior, which is needed in the comparison.

However, if the two Hebrew words are written together, the first consonant can be taken as the preposition meaning "like," and the rest of the word can be related to a Ugaritic word meaning "glaze." In a passage dealing with the problem of immortality, Aqhat has this to say concerning humankind's old age and mortality:

> Glaze will be poured on my head,
>> plaster (or potash) upon my head.
> And I will die as everyone dies;
>> I too will surely die.[12]

The Ugaritic word for "glaze" is *spsg*, and this word seems to be hidden in the proverb. Kitchen summarizes and applies the data as follows:

> In Proverbs 26:23, there occurs the *crux interpretatum*, "silver dross" *(kesep-sigim)*, in the context, "Silver dross overlaid upon an earthen pot are fervent lips and a wicked heart." This can now be read as *kĕ-sapsag-mi* [treating -*m* as an enclitic *mêm*], "Like glaze," and the whole sentence be rendered:
> "Like glaze coated upon an earthen pot, are fervent lips with a wicked heart."

The word *sapsag* for "glaze" first turned up in Ugaritic
(spsg) and has received independent confirmation from
Hittite documents (in the form, *zapzagai-*, and variants).[13]

Of course, an earthen vessel overlaid with glaze is precisely what the context requires.[14] Perhaps it should be
added that there is now archaeological evidence that
pottery was glazed in the Holy Land at that time. Specifically, glaze was laid over a core of crushed quartz.[15]

Incidentally, the NIV (accepting the different Hebrew
word division) renders the proverb this way:

> Like a coating of glaze over earthenware
> are fervent lips with an evil heart.

Another case of a possibly incorrect word division
may occur in Amos 6:12, where the scribal confusion is
not fission, but evidently the fusion of two words into
one. Here "Does one plow there with oxen?" should
probably be read "Does one plow the sea with oxen?"[16]
One more probable case of scribal confusion may be
found in Psalm 42:5–6. Most scholars agree that Psalms
42–43 were originally one psalm (in many Hebrew MSS
they comprise one psalm; see also any good exegetical
commentary on the Hebrew text). One of the arguments
for their original unity is the refrain in 42:5, 11; 43:5.
The refrain is virtually identical in all three references
except for the last line of 42:5 (MT 42:6). But when one
combines the first word of 42:6 (MT 42:7) with the end
of 42:5, one discovers what almost certainly happened.
In all three occurrences of the refrain, the last poetic
line of the Hebrew text reads (without vowel points):

> *yšw ʿwt pnyw ʾlhy*
> *yšw ʿwt pny w ʾlhy*
> *yšw ʿwt pny w ʾlhy*

Now if one moves what is presently the third masculine singular pronominal suffix in the first line above
from "his face" to "my God," then it too will read *yšw ʿwt
pny w ʾlhy*, thus making all three lines identical, with the
same sense. Most scholars concur that a scribe was guilty
of a wrong word division in the first reference, and that
the *w* should be read as a conjunction at the beginning
of the next word. Significantly, a few Hebrew MSS, the
Greek Septuagint, and the Syriac Peshitta have this reading. Regarding the ultimate meaning and translation,
the Hebrew says literally "the salvation of my face and
my God." "The salvation of my face" is simply a Hebrew
idiom for "the One who saves me," that is, "my Savior";
hence, for the whole line, "my Savior and my God" (NIV).

Perhaps this is also the most appropriate place to say a
brief word about the *tiqqune sopherim* ("corrections of/by
the scribes"), referred to in the NIV preface (quoted at the
outset of this chapter) as "the ancient scribal traditions
relating to textual changes." There are footnotes concerning several of these readings at Genesis 18:22; Judges
18:30; 1 Samuel 3:13; 2 Samuel 12:14; Job 7:20; 32:3;
Jeremiah 2:11; Hosea 4:7 (twice). CBT accepted such
scribal readings in Judges 18:30; Job 7:20; Hosea 4:7 (in
only the first case here), but in each of these instances
there was additional support from other textual witnesses.

These illustrations of Waltke's fourth textual rule
above are the exceptions that prove the general rule that
the NIV adhered rather rigidly to the MT.[17]

The New Testament

What was the textual basis of the NIV New Testament?
The question is answered briefly in the preface to the NIV:

> The Greek text used in translating the New Testament
> was an eclectic one. No other piece of ancient literature

has such an abundance of manuscript witnesses as does the New Testament. Where existing manuscripts differ, the translators made their choice of readings according to accepted principles of New Testament textual criticism. Footnotes call attention to places where there was uncertainty about what the original text was. The best current printed texts of the Greek New Testament were used.

Several sentences in this summary call for further comment. For instance, what is meant by an "eclectic" Greek text of the New Testament? "Because [most textual] scholars 'gather out' their readings from a variety of texts, their approach is usually called 'eclectic.'"[18] In that approach the textual specialist prefers one reading over the others on a case-by-case basis. "He examines all the variations in each variation unit to determine what reading is the one from which the others most likely deviated."[19]

To answer the question more completely, it is necessary to introduce the various text-types or manuscript families. Most textual witnesses (primarily Greek MSS and papyrus fragments, the ancient versions, and Scripture quotations by the early church fathers) can be grouped into one of three major text-types according to the variant readings occurring in them:

1. The *Alexandrian text-type* was so named because it apparently emerged in and around Alexandria, Egypt. It is represented by the majority of the *early* papyri readings (introduced in the literature by P); by several *early* uncial MSS (in capital letters), including ℵ (Sinaiticus), B (Vaticanus), and C (Ephraemi Rescriptus); by the Coptic versions; and by significant Alexandrian church fathers, such as Clement and Origen.

2. The *Western text-type* is represented by the uncial MS D (Bezae), the Old Latin, the Old Syriac, and the church fathers Irenaeus, Tertullian, and Jerome. Most

scholars are reluctant to follow readings that have only Western support.

3. "The *Byzantine text* is represented by the vast majority of Greek MSS and most of the later church fathers. This text was largely preserved in the area of the old Byzantine empire, which is now Turkey, Bulgaria, Greece, Albania, and the former Yugoslavia."[20] It is significant that "no ante-Nicene Father quotes a distinctively Syrian [= Byzantine] reading."[21]

The so-called *Caesarean text-type* (found only in the Gospels) is now sometimes referred to as "other important witnesses."[22]

The "accepted principles" (see the quotation from the preface to the NIV above) that go with such external MS evidence include the following: (1) Generally, the earlier MSS are preferred. To illustrate, in Luke 8:43 the NIV reads, "And a woman was there who had been subject to bleeding for twelve years, but no one could heal her." The NIV textual note, however, points out that many MSS add, "and she had spent all she had on doctors." "This fits well the tendency of scribes to harmonize the various accounts. Here it is most likely that a scribe added this statement to make Luke more like Mark 5:26."[23] Burdick further explains, "Since the clause was omitted by our best uncial manuscript, the Vaticanus, and by the Bodmer papyrus (P 75), which dates about A.D. 200, the NIV translators also omitted it [though preserving it in the footnote]."[24] Doubtless one of the reasons for the general preference for older MSS is that the early papyrus fragments of the New Testament discovered in the twentieth century have often supported readings in the great Alexandrian MSS, Vaticanus and Sinaiticus.[25] In fact, P52 (containing John 18:31–34, 37–38) possibly dates as early as A.D. 100–115—only twenty to thirty years removed from the original text by the apostle.

(2) Normally, the reading supported in widely separated geographical areas is preferred. This principle is so obvious that it requires no illustration. (3) The reading supported by the greatest number of text-types is usually preferred. This principle is also patently true.

In addition to the three principles just mentioned, there are others that go with internal evidence. Here, the most important is that the reading that best explains the origin of the others should be favored. For instance, in the example above involving Luke 8:43, "It is far more likely that the clause was borrowed from Mark 5:26. If it had been original, it is difficult to explain why the clause would have been dropped by the scribes of P75 B [Vaticanus] D [Bezae]."[26] So the NIV reading in Luke 8:43 has both external (MS) and internal (intrinsic probability) evidence in its favor.

This broad principle concerning internal evidence has several corollaries: (1) The shorter reading is usually preferred. The known tendency of scribes was to expand for various reasons, often because of harmonization. Again, this would support the shorter reading in Luke 8:43. There is an obvious exception to this rule when it is clear that there has been an inadvertent omission, as in Matthew 5:19. Here some MSS omit verse 19b because the scribe's eyes came back to the second occurrence of "heaven" instead of the first, thus skipping the intervening material.

(2) Normally, the more difficult reading is preferred. On the part of some scribes, there was a tendency to smooth out difficulties. One such example is John 1:18, where a literal rendering of the reference to the second person of the Trinity would be "the one and only [i.e., unique] God." Although some MSS read "Son," the MS evidence favors "God" over "Son." All the earliest MSS and papyri, supported by other ancient witnesses, read "God." The latter reading would also form an inclusio, in that John's prologue would have begun (v. 1) and ended (v. 18) with a ref-

erence to Christ as "God." Greenlee adds that "it is also clearly the harder reading."[27] Thus it is probably correct.

(3) The reading that best accords with the writer's style and vocabulary is preferred. This principle is self-explanatory and almost "goes without saying."

(4) Generally, the reading that best fits the context and/or the writer's theology is preferred. This principle is transparently evident, requiring no elaboration.

(5) In parallel passages the less harmonious reading is usually preferred because of the scribal tendency to harmonize. To illustrate, The KJV "Onlyite" Gail Riplinger claims that the KJV calls for the Christian to "take up his cross," but that new versions "omit" this clause.[28] She does not identify the passage, but she is referring to Mark 10:21. The KJV actually has "come, take up the cross, and follow me," whereas the NIV reads simply "come, follow me." She fails to indicate that the "omitted" clause occurs in both the KJV *and the NIV* in Matthew 16:24; Mark 8:34; Luke 9:23. The NIV translates Mark 8:34: "If anyone would come after me, he must deny himself and take up his cross and follow me."

The reason for the alleged omission is not because of some New Age conspiracy, as Riplinger charges. Rather, the real reason for the NIV reading is that the earliest Greek MSS of the New Testament do not have the clause in Mark 10:21. It seems clear that a copyist inserted it here from 8:34. The shorter reading not only has better MS support but also is the less harmonious reading and so is preferred for that reason as well. If the clause had been "omitted" because of a conspiracy to remove taking up the cross from the cost of Christian discipleship, why does the NIV retain it in the other three Gospel references mentioned above?[29]

At the practical level, in conservative-evangelical circles the debate over the best Greek text of the New Testament focuses on three main options:

1. Follow the Textus Receptus (TR, "received text"), the Greek text that lies behind the KJV. As I have indicated elsewhere, however, this position suffers from the fact that it strongly implies that knowledge in the fields of Bible translation work and textual studies ceased in 1611.[30] The argument from providential preservation has sometimes been employed to support the TR, but Johnson objects:

> (4) Fourth, the claim that the Textus Receptus type of text has been *preserved providentially* as the true text of God's people through the ages is not valid. It was not the text of the early church in Egypt, nor in Palestine, nor in the West. Jerome, using the available Greek manuscripts and the Old Latin, gave Western Christians the Vulgate, a text much closer to the Alexandrian text-type than to the Textus Receptus. And the Christians of the West certainly had just as much a claim to be the people of God as did those of Constantinople.
>
> (5) Fifth, the Textus Receptus type of text itself is not a uniform text. For example, Colwell has identified "families" among these very cursives that are supposed to be directly descended from the autographa (cf. Acts 20:28). The lack of consensus among the cursives in Revelation is the most obvious example of this. What becomes, then, of the argument from providence?
>
> To conclude, may we not advance the claim that God in His providence has allowed us to recover the early Alexandrian type of manuscripts to enable us to come to a clearer text? To discover that the earliest of our New Testament manuscripts, such as P46, P66 and P75, give us essentially the *same text as that of Vaticanus and Sinaiticus*, manuscripts later by almost two centuries, should be cause for renewed confidence in the text of such later witnesses.[31]

Wallace has written a lengthy article demonstrating the weakness of the argument from providential preservation.[32]

It is somewhat ironic that Dean J.W. Burgon, whose work is praised by TR "Onlyites," would not agree with their position, for he wrote:

> Once and for all, we request it may be clearly understood that we do not, by any means, claim *perfection* for the Received Text. We entertain no extravagant notions on this subject. Again and again we shall have occasion to point out . . . that the *Textus Receptus* needs correction.[33]

Sometimes KJV Only (and TR Only) adherents allege that modern versions such as the NIV downplay the deity of Christ in their "new" and different textual readings. Carson, however, presents a chart demonstrating that the actual situation is precisely the opposite.[34]

2. Follow the readings of the majority of MSS (the Majority Text).[35] The Majority Text must be distinguished from the TR referred to above, because Wallace has counted 1,838 differences between the two.[36] Wallace has also produced a chart showing that the Byzantine/Majority text-type is not attested in the first three centuries and that it did not become a majority until the ninth century. Here is his chart:[37]

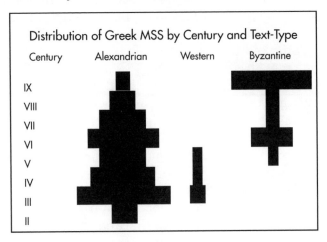

Distribution of Greek MSS by Century and Text-Type

| Century | Alexandrian | Western | Byzantine |

As the chart makes clear, the oldest text-type (as far as extant witnesses are concerned) is the Alexandrian, the second oldest is the Western, and the third oldest is the Byzantine/Majority. Wallace concludes, "The Greek MSS, versions and Church fathers provide a threefold cord not easily broken. . . . There is simply no shred of evidence that the Byzantine text-type existed prior to the fourth century."[38] Pickering attempted to build a case for its existence earlier than the fourth century.[39] Carson, Wallace, and Fee, however, have adequately refuted his case.[40] Sturz likewise attempted to prove that the Byzantine text-type was earlier than usually thought.[41] Yet Metzger concluded his review of Sturz's work, "One must also ask whether the evidence of this or that Byzantine *reading* among the early papyri demonstrates the existence of the Byzantine *text-type* . . . One is led to conclude, therefore, that Sturz has failed to prove that the Byzantine text-type is older than the fourth century."[42]

The approach that relies wholly on majority readings also runs counter to another widely accepted general principle of textual criticism: Manuscripts are to be weighed, not merely counted. This means that preference should be given to those MSS that have most often proved to be correct when all the other tests (both external and internal) have been applied to them. The MSS that come out ahead when this principle is followed belong most frequently to the Alexandrian text-type.

Kohlenberger provides some final "food for thought" for this approach: "If the basic argument that the 'majority rules' were applied consistently, the Latin Vulgate would be our Bible! Latin MSS outnumber Greek about eight thousand to five thousand, and the Latin Bible has centuries more dominance in the church than all English versions combined" (including the KJV!).[43]

3. Follow a reasoned eclectic approach (described above in connection with external and internal evidence

and the major text-types). The vast majority of specialists in Greek and New Testament (including the most conservative ones) subscribe to this approach. This is so much the case that Lewis, in evaluating the NKJV New Testament, remarks, "The NKJV is a deliberate effort to turn the processes of scholarship back to the state of textual knowledge prior to the influence of Westcott–Hort. . . . This publication reconstructed as closely as possible the Greek text underlying the KJV as revised in 1769 by Benjamin Blayney."[44] He concludes, "One must ask if this championing of the Received Text's superiority (or even the Majority Text's) is a step forward or is the last gasp in traditionalism's dying struggle to maintain itself. . . . The basic question is not what was or was not in the KJV but what the original writers wrote."[45] An eclectic approach, then, seems to have the support of most of the data of textual criticism, appears to be the most balanced and scientific method, and was the approach followed by CBT for the NIV.[46]

To keep things in proper perspective, however, it must be remembered that, though no two MSS are completely identical, all Greek MSS and papyri agree on approximately 98 percent of the New Testament Greek text. The substantive differences, then, pertain to about 2 percent of the total text of the New Testament. In fact, thanks to the practice of New Testament textual criticism, the number of still uncertain readings can be reduced to half a page. And the differences do not affect Christian doctrines. They are still intact.

Even though the NKJV follows the Greek text of the KJV New Testament (the TR) instead of the Byzantine/Majority text-type, its preface expresses a balanced perspective on such textual differences:

> Differences among the Greek manuscripts of the New Testament such as omission or inclusion of a word or a

clause, and two paragraphs in the Gospels, should not overshadow the overwhelming degree of *agreement* which exists among the ancient records. . . . Readers may be assured that textual debate does not affect one in a thousand words of the Greek New Testament. Furthermore, no established doctrine is called into question by any doubts about the correct reading in this or that text. The Christian can approach his New Testament with confidence.[47]

So a good translation will have a balanced textual basis.[48]

4

A Balanced
Translation Philosophy

What types of Bible translations are there? What kind is the NIV? Where does it fit among all the others? Bible translators and linguists speak primarily of two major types of translations. The first is referred to variously as formal, complete, literal, or gloss equivalence. Here the translator pursues a word-for-word rendering as much as possible. The New American Standard Bible (NASB) and the New King James Version (NKJV) are good examples of this approach.

Fortunately it is frequently possible to translate literally and still retain contemporary English idiom and excellent literary style. Indeed, literally thousands of such renderings occur in the NIV, beginning with the first verse of the Bible. "In the beginning God created the heavens and the earth" is a straightforward translation of the Hebrew text of Genesis 1:1, and it is also good English. So why change it? In fact, why not follow this more literal approach everywhere and all the time, with an absolute minimum of interpretation? Silva responds, "Translators who view their work as pure renderings rather than interpretations only delude themselves; indeed, if they could achieve some kind of noninterpretative rendering, their work would be completely useless."[1] Taylor reinforces the point: "All translation is interpretation, as George Steiner and others have pointed out.

At every point, the translator is required to interpret, evaluate, judge, and choose."[2]

Silva further indicates that a "successful translation requires (1) mastery of the source language—certainly a much more sophisticated knowledge than one can acquire over a period of four or five years; (2) superb interpretation skills and breadth of knowledge so as not to miss the nuances of the original; and (3) a very high aptitude for writing in the target language so as to express accurately both the cognitive and the affective elements of the message."[3] And Speiser reminds us that

> The main task of a translator is to keep faith with two different masters, one at the source and the other at the receiving end. . . . If he is unduly swayed by the original, and substitutes word for word rather than idiom for idiom, he is traducing what he should be translating, to the detriment of both source and target. And if he veers too far in the opposite direction, by favoring the second medium at the expense of the first, the result is a paraphrase.[4]

He concludes by declaring that a "faithful translation is by no means the same thing as a literal rendering."[5]

Unfortunately, then, it is often not possible to translate literally and retain natural, idiomatic, clear English. Consider the NASB rendering of Matthew 13:20: "The one on whom seed was sown on the rocky places, this is the man who hears the word and immediately receives it with joy." The NIV reads: "The one who received the seed that fell on rocky places is the man who hears the word and at once receives it with joy." Here the NASB is so woodenly literal that the result is a cumbersome, awkward, poorly constructed sentence. The NIV, on the other hand, has a natural and smooth style without sacrificing accuracy.

The second major type of translation is referred to variously as dynamic, functional, gloss, or idiomatic equivalence. Here the translator attempts a thought-for-thought rendering. The Good News Bible (GNB; also known as Today's English Version, TEV), the New Living Translation (NLT), God's Word, and the Contemporary English Version (CEV) are some examples of this approach to the translation task. Such versions seek to find the best modern cultural equivalent that will have the same effect the original message had in its ancient cultures. Obviously this approach is a much freer one.

At this point the reader may be surprised that the NIV has not been included as an illustration of either of these two major types of translations. The reason is that, in my opinion, it fits neither. After considerable personal study, comparison, and analysis, I have become totally convinced that in order to do complete justice to translations like the NIV and the New Revised Standard Version (NRSV), scholars simply must recognize the validity of a third major category of translation: the balanced or mediating type. If we are to discuss this subject intelligently, we must have a working definition of formal equivalence and dynamic equivalence. To achieve this, I quote at length from Nida:

> Since "there are . . . no such things as identical equivalents". . . , one must in translating seek to find the closest possible equivalent. However, there are fundamentally two different types of equivalence: one which may be called formal and another which is primarily dynamic.
>
> Formal equivalence focuses attention on the message itself, in both form and content. . . . Viewed from this formal orientation, one is concerned that the message in the receptor language should match as closely as possible the different elements in the source language. This means . . . that the message in the receptor culture is constantly com-

pared with the message in the source culture to determine standards of accuracy and correctness.

The type of translation which most closely typifies this structural equivalence might be called a "gloss translation," in which the translator attempts to reproduce as literally and meaningfully as possible the form and content of the original. . . . [Student] needs call for a relatively close approximation to the structure of the early . . . text, both as to form (e.g. syntax and idioms) and content (e.g. themes and concepts). Such a translation would require numerous footnotes in order to make the text fully comprehensible.

A gloss translation of this type is designed to permit the reader to identify himself as fully as possible with a person in the source-language context, and to understand as much as he can of the customs, manner of thought, and means of expression. For example, a phrase such as "holy kiss" (Romans 16:16) in a gloss translation would be rendered literally, and would probably be supplemented with a footnote explaining that this was a customary method of greeting in New Testament times.

In contrast, a translation which attempts to produce a dynamic rather than a formal equivalence is based upon "the principle of equivalent effect." . . . In such a translation one is not so concerned with matching the receptor-language message with the source-language message, but with the dynamic relationship . . . , that the relationship between receptor and message should be substantially the same as that which existed between the original receptors and the message.

A translation of dynamic equivalence aims at complete naturalness of expression, and tries to relate the receptor to modes of behavior relevant within the context of his own culture; it does not insist that he understand the cultural patterns of the source-language context in order to comprehend the message. Of course, there are varying degrees of such dynamic-equivalence translations. . . . [Phillips, e.g.,] seeks for equivalent effect. . . . In Romans 16:16 he quite naturally translates "greet one another with a holy kiss" as "give one another a hearty handshake all around."

Between the two poles of translating (i.e. between strict formal equivalence and complete dynamic equivalence) there are a number of intervening grades, representing various acceptable standards of literary translating.[6]

Greenstein further describes the principle of dynamic equivalence as proposing a "three-stage translation process: analysis of the expression in the source language to determine its meaning, transfer of this meaning to the target language, and restructuring of the meaning in the world of expression of the target language."[7]

Two observations may be helpful at this point. First, it is instructive that the NIV retains "Greet one another with a holy kiss" in Romans 16:16. Second, it is significant that Nida seems to open the door for a mediating position between the two main translation philosophies, theories, or methods. In general terms, all Bible translation is simply "the process of beginning with something (written or oral) in one language (the source language) and expressing it in another language (the receptor language)."[8] A translation cannot be said to be faithful that does not pay adequate attention to both the source language and the receptor language.

A distinction must be made between dynamic equivalence as a translation principle and dynamic equivalence as a translation philosophy. The latter exists only when a version sets out to produce a dynamic-equivalence rendering from start to finish, as the GNB did. The foreword to the *Special Edition Good News Bible,* with features by Lion (England), indicates that "word-for-word translation does not accurately convey the force of the original, so the GNB uses instead the 'dynamic equivalent', the words which will have the same force and meaning today as the original text had for its first readers." Dynamic equivalence as a translation principle, on the other hand, is used in varying degrees by all versions of the Bible.[9] This is easily illustrated by a few selected examples.[10]

A "literal" rendering of the opening part of the Hebrew text of Isaiah 40:2 would read: "Speak to the heart of Jerusalem." Yet all English versions (including the KJV) see the need for a dynamic-equivalence translation here (e.g., the NIV has "Speak tenderly to Jerusalem").

In Jeremiah 2:2 the KJV and the NASB read "in the ears of Jerusalem," but the NKJV and the NIV have "in the hearing of Jerusalem." Here the NKJV is just as "dynamic" as the NIV. That it did not have to be is clear from the NASB. Yet it wanted to communicate the meaning in a natural way to modern readers, which is precisely what the NIV also wanted to do.

In Haggai 2:16 the NASB has "grain heap," but the KJV, NKJV, and NIV all use "heap" alone (which is all the Hebrew has). Here the formal-equivalent version, the NASB, is freer than the NIV, which is alleged by some to adhere to the dynamic-equivalence method.

The KJV and the NKJV read "no power at all" in John 19:11, whereas the NIV has only "no power" (in accord with the Greek). Which version is following the formal-equivalence approach here, and which ones are following the dynamic approach?

One could continue ad infinitum with this kind of illustration. Suffice it to mention additionally that there is a published book over two hundred pages long that is a glossary to the oddities of the KJV word use and diction.[11] In a similar vein, Youngblood has written:

> To render the Greek word *sarx* by "flesh" virtually every time it appears does not require the services of a translator; all one needs is a dictionary (or, better yet, a

computer). But to recognize that *sarx* has differing connotations in different contexts, that in addition to "flesh" it often means "human standards" or "earthly descent" or "sinful nature" or "sexual impulse" or "person," etc., and therefore to translate *sarx* in a variety of ways, is to understand that translation is not only a mechanical, word-for-word process but also a nuanced [I would have said contextually nuanced], thought-for-thought procedure. Translation, as any expert in the field will readily admit, is just as much an art as it is a science. Word-for-word translations typically demonstrate great respect for the source language . . . but often pay only lip service to the requirements of the target language. . . .

When translators of Scripture insist on reproducing every lexical and grammatical element in their English renderings, the results are often grotesque.[12]

What kind of translation, then, is the NIV? Where does it fit? While these and related questions have been dealt with generally in several publications and reviews, they are addressed specifically in only one published, authoritative source by the NIV translators themselves:

Broadly speaking, there are several methods of translation: the concordant one, which ranges from literalism to the comparative freedom of the King James Version and even more of the Revised Standard Version, both of which follow the syntactical structure of the Hebrew and Greek texts as far as is compatible with good English; the paraphrastic one, in which the translator restates the gist of the text in his own words; and the method of equivalence, in which the translator seeks to understand as fully as possible what the biblical writers had to say (a criterion common, of course, to the careful use of any method) and then tries to find its closest equivalent in contemporary usage. In its more advanced form this is spoken of as dynamic equivalence, in which the translator seeks to express the meaning as the biblical writers would if they were writing in English today. All these methods have their values when responsibly used.

As for the NIV, its method is an *eclectic* one with the emphasis for the most part on a *flexible use of concordance and equivalence,* but with a *minimum of literalism, paraphrase, or outright dynamic equivalence.* In other words, the NIV stands on *middle ground*—by no means the easiest position to occupy. It may fairly be said that the translators were convinced that, through long patience in seeking the right words, it is possible to attain a high degree of faithfulness in putting into clear and idiomatic English what the Hebrew and Greek texts say. Whatever literary distinction the NIV has is the result of the persistence with which this course was pursued.[13]

Elsewhere I have written:

About two thousand years ago, when confronted with the prospect of translating Plato's *Protagoras* into Latin, Cicero declared, "It is hard to preserve in a translation the charm of expressions which in another language are most felicitous. . . . If I render word for word, the result will sound uncouth, and if compelled by necessity I alter anything in the order or wording, I shall seem to have departed from the function of a translator." Such is the dilemma of all translators! And the problem is particularly acute for those who attempt to translate the Bible, for it is the eternal Word of God. The goal, of course, is to be as faithful as possible in all renderings. But faithfulness is a double-edged sword, for true faithfulness in translation means being faithful not only to the original language but also to the "target" or "receptor" language. That is precisely what we attempted to produce in the New International Version—just the right balance between accuracy and the best contemporary idiom.[14]

In spite of that goal, I am certain that from time to time we will continue to be criticized by some for being literal but not contemporary enough, and by others for being contemporary but not literal enough. Yet perhaps that fact in itself will indicate that we have basically succeeded.

All this clearly indicates that CBT attempted to make the NIV a balanced, mediating version—one that would fall about halfway between the most literal and the most free. But is that, in fact, where the NIV fits? There are many neutral parties who think it is. For example, Sheeley and Nash state, "The NIV committees attempted to walk this fine line, and, to their credit, usually achieved a good sense of balance between fidelity to the ancient texts and sensitivity to modern expression."[15] They conclude:

> Like any other modern translation of the Bible, the NIV should not be considered the *only* true translation. Its great achievement, though, lies in its readability. No other modern English translation has reached the same level and still maintained such a close connection to the ancient languages.[16]

A similar opinion is expressed in the *Report to General Synod Abbotsford 1995* by the Committee on Bible Translations appointed by Synod Lincoln 1992 of the Canadian Reformed Churches. The members of the Committee are P. Aasman, J. Geertsema, W. Smouter, C. Van Dam, and G.H. Visscher. They thoroughly and carefully investigated the NASB, the NKJV, and the NIV. They indicated that the NIV "attempted to strike a balance between a high degree of faithfulness to the text and clarity for the receptor in the best possible English."[17] A section of their Report analyzed the NIV as "balancing fluency and accuracy."[18]

They added that "it was frequently our experience that very often when our initial reaction to an NIV translation was negative, further study and investigation convinced us that the NIV translators had taken into account all the factors involved and had actually rendered the best possible translation of the three versions."[19] Similarly, "Our Committee often questioned a passage in the NIV as being too interpretive, but upon closer examination it was often discovered that the NIV had produced a text that was accurate yet idiomatic."[20] They concluded that "the NIV is more idiomatic than the NASB and NKJV, but at the same time, as accurate as the NASB and NKJV."[21] Numerous NIV users have expressed the same sentiments as this Committee did in its report. Incidentally, the General Synod Abbotsford 1995 of the Canadian Reformed Churches adopted these two recommendations (among many others):

> B. To continue to recommend the NIV for use in the churches.
> C. To continue to leave it in the freedom of the churches if they feel compelled to use other translations that received favourable reviews in the reports.[22]

Another neutral voice is that of Terry White in an article about how a Baptist General Conference church (Wooddale in Eden Prairie, Minn.) endorsed the NIV as the best translation for their membership. The church appointed a task force to evaluate the NIV, the RSV, the NASB, and the NKJV. The NIV came out ahead in nine of ten areas evaluated (most readable, best scholarship used, best grammatically, best paragraphing, best concordances and supplemental writing, best for use by laity, best Old Testament, best New Testament, and best total Bible). A slight edge was given to the NASB as the most accurate rendering of the original texts. Nonetheless, it was clear that the NIV had the best overall balance.[23]

Strictly speaking, then, the NIV is not a dynamic-equivalence translation. If it were, it would read "snakes will no longer be dangerous" (GNB) instead of "dust will be the serpent's food" (Isa. 65:25). Or it would read in 1 Samuel 20:30 "You bastard!" (GNB) instead of "You son of a perverse and rebellious woman!" Similar illustrations could be multiplied to demonstrate that the NIV is an idiomatically balanced translation.

How was such a balance achieved? By having a built-in system of checks and balances. We called it the A-B-C-D's of the NIV, using those letters as an alphabetic acrostic to represent *accuracy, beauty, clarity,* and *dignity.* We wanted to be *accurate,* that is, as faithful to the original text as possible. But it is also important to be equally faithful to the target or receptor language—English in this case. So we did not want to make the mistake—in the name of *accuracy*—of creating "translation English" that would not be *beautiful* and natural. *Accuracy,* then, must be balanced by *beauty* of language. CBT attempted to make the NIV read and flow the way any great English literature should. Calvin D. Linton (professor emeritus of English Literature and dean emeritus of the College of Arts and Sciences at George Washington University) has praised the *beauty* of the NIV as literature:

> The NIV is filled with sensitive renderings of rhythms, from the exultant beat of the Song of Deborah and Barak (Judg. 5:1–31) to the "dying fall" of the rhythms of the world-weary Teacher in Ecclesiastes, with myriad effects in between. As a random sample, let the reader *speak* the following lines from Job (29:2–3), being careful to give full value to the difference between stressed and unstressed syllables:
>
> > How I long for the months gone by,
> >   for the days when God watched over me,
> > when his lamp shone upon my head
> >   and by his light I walked through darkness!
>
> It is better than the KJV![24]

At the same time we did not want to make the mistake—in the name of *beauty*—of creating lofty, flowery English that would not be *clear*. So *beauty* must be balanced by *clarity:* "When a high percentage of people misunderstand a rendering, it cannot be regarded as a legitimate translation."[25] If a translation is to be both *accurate* and *clear* (idiomatic), it cannot be a mechanical exercise; instead, it must be a highly nuanced process. Godfrey Smith wrote in *The Sunday Times* (London):

> I was won over by the way the new Bible [the NIV] handles Paul's magnificent [First] Epistle to the Corinthians [13:4]. "Charity suffereth long, and is kind; charity envieth not; charity vaunteth not itself, is not puffed up." So runs the old version [the KJV], but the word charity is a real show-stopper. The new version puts it with admirable simplicity: "Love is patient, love is kind. It does not envy, it does not boast, it is not proud." The old thunder has been lost, but the gain in sense is enormous.[26]

My favorite illustration of lack of *clarity* is the KJV rendering of Job 36:33: "The noise thereof sheweth concerning it, the cattle also concerning the vapour." In the interests of *clarity* the NIV reads: "His [God's] thunder announces the coming storm; even the cattle make known its approach." Or consider the Lord's description of the leviathan in Job 41:12–14 (KJV): "I will not conceal his parts, nor his power, nor his comely proportion. Who can discover the face of his garment? or who can come to him with his double bridle? Who can open the doors of his face? his teeth are terrible round about." Again, in order to communicate *clearly* in contemporary English idiom, the NIV translates:

> I will not fail to speak of his limbs,
>   his strength and his graceful form.

Who can strip off his outer coat?
   Who would approach him with a bridle?
Who dares open the doors of his mouth,
   ringed about with his fearsome teeth?

My favorite bumper sticker for translators is "ESCHEW OBFUSCATION." Such obfuscation is effectively illustrated by the following true story from Allison Sanders in the *Houston Chronicle*:

> The father of a Houston, Texas, high-school pupil received this message from the school principal inviting him to a meeting about a new educational program:
> "Our school's Cross-Graded, Multi-Ethnic, Individualized Learning Program is designed to enhance the concept of an Open-Ended Learning Program with emphasis on a continuum of multi-ethnic academically enriched learning, using the identified intellectually gifted child as the agent or director of his own learning. Major emphasis is on cross-graded, multi-ethnic learning with the main objective being to learn respect for the uniqueness of a person."
> This was followed by two more paragraphs in the same strange language.
> The father wrote back: "I have a college degree, speak two foreign languages and four Indian dialects, have been to a number of county fairs and three Mexican goat ropings, and make my living as a wordsmith, but I haven't the faintest idea as to what . . . you are talking about. Do you?"[27]

The importance of *clarity* in Bible translations is obvious. On the other hand, CBT did not want to make the mistake—in the name of *clarity*—of stooping to slang, vulgarisms, street vernacular, and unnecessarily undignified language. *Clarity,* then, must be balanced by *dignity,* particularly since one of our objectives was to produce a general, all-church-use Bible. Some of the dynamic-equivalence versions are at times unnecessarily *undignified,* as illustrated above in 1 Samuel 20:30.

Additional examples could be given. But the point is that when we produced the NIV, we wanted *accuracy,* but not at the expense of *beauty;* we wanted *beauty,* but not at the expense of *clarity;* and we wanted *clarity,* but not at the expense of *dignity.* We wanted all these in a nice *balance.* Did we succeed? Rather than restrict oneself to descriptive terms like formal equivalence, dynamic equivalence, paraphrase, and so on, in answering this question, it is perhaps even more helpful to perceive the distinctions Callow and Beekman make among four types of translations: highly literal, modified literal, idiomatic, and unduly free. Their view may be diagrammed like this:[28]

Unacceptable	Acceptable Types		Unacceptable
highly literal	modified literal	idiomatic	unduly free

In their classification system the NIV, in my opinion, contains primarily modified literal and idiomatic renderings, although with a greater number of idiomatic ones.

To sum up, there is need for a new category in classifying translations—a classification called *mediating* position. What I have in mind may be demonstrated visually by the chart below. It contains only what I regard as major, standard, committee-produced translations. That automatically excludes works like the Living Bible and the Message. Also excluded are versions below a sixth-grade reading level, such as the CEV, the NCV, and the NIrV (see the list of abbreviations for the explanation of these and other abbreviations). The latter are not general, all-church-use Bibles (in my estimation). Incidentally, the NIV is placed at a reading level of 7.8, which is virtually identical with the average reading level of U.S. adults.[29]

So a good translation will follow a balanced translation philosophy.

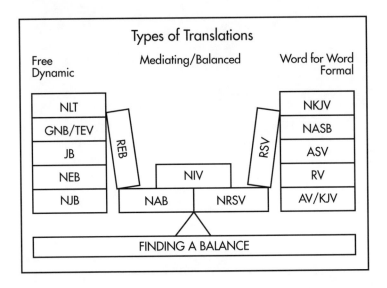

5

A Balanced Solution to Difficulties

How should Bible translators handle difficult passages? Some KJV-Only advocates attack all modern versions because of alleged problems or difficulties they are said to create when compared with the KJV. Lewis, however, notes that the "same sort of attacks that are now made on new translations were made on the KJV when it was new. If the same kind of fine-tooth combing that is now expended on the new translations is used on the KJV, we see that the problems of the KJV are as numerous and as serious as those of the new translations. The need for new translations lies in the inadequacies of the KJV."[1]

One of the balanced ways CBT approached such problems in translating the NIV was to recognize viable alternative solutions and renderings through the use of "Or" text notes (as well as other kinds of translator footnotes). Over fifty selected examples from the Old Testament and fifteen from the New will suffice to illustrate the point.

Genesis 6:3

One kind of problem translators face is a semantic one—determining the right nuance to assign to a Hebrew or Greek word in a specific context. Such a difficulty is found in Genesis 6:3. The main NIV text reads: "Then the LORD said, 'My Spirit will not contend with man forever, for he is mortal; his days will be a hundred and twenty years.'" This seems to indicate that there would be a 120-

year period of grace between God's announcement of coming judgment and the actual beginning of the flood itself (v. 17; 7:11–16; cf. Heb. 11:7; 1 Peter 3:20; 2 Peter 2:5). The "Or" footnotes, on the other hand, provide an alternative: "Then the Lord said, 'My spirit will not remain in man forever, for he is corrupt. . . .'" This seems to announce that, after the flood, the human life span would be progressively shortened and eventually limited to 120 years (see 11:10–26; Deut. 34:7). Since a good case can be made for both options (see the commentaries), CBT presents both in the interests of balance.

Genesis 8:21

Sometimes it is difficult to decide the particular syntactical function of Hebrew and Greek connectives. A case in point is whether Hebrew *kî* in Genesis 8:21 introduces a concessive clause or a causal/explanatory clause. The NIV offers concessive in the text ("even though") and causal/explanatory in the footnote alternative ("for"). In the former, the sense would be that the Lord would never again curse the ground because of humans *in spite of* the fact that they showed no improvement after the flood. In the latter, the *reason* for such a decision by the Lord is *explained*. It is *because* humanity is incurably evil and human nature had not changed after the flood (see 6:5), leaving the door open for God to solve the problem ultimately "freely by his grace through the redemption that came by Christ Jesus" (Rom. 3:24). As von Rad puts it, "The same condition, which . . . is the basis for God's judgment, . . . reveals God's grace and providence."[2] Again, the NIV's balanced approach allows for the possibility of either syntactical usage.

Genesis 10:2, 8; 1 Chronicles 1:5, 10; Daniel 5:2, 22

Probably most Bible readers are not aware of the full semantic range of the Hebrew words for "son" and "father." So CBT furnishes translator footnotes on the above references reminding the reader that Hebrew *bēn* may not mean "son" here but "grandson," "descendant," "successor," or "nation," and *ʾāb* may not mean "father" but "grandfather," "ancestor," "predecessor," or "founder." In analyzing genres of literature like the table of nations and genealogies (such as those in Gen. 5; 11; 1 Chron. 1–9), it is important to remember these semantic options since there can be gaps of as many as six consecutive names (e.g., in Ezra 7:3 between Azariah and Meraioth when one compares that list with 1 Chron. 6:6–11, demonstrating that Azariah is the "descendant" of Meraioth, not the immediate "son" of Meraioth). Similar gaps occur in the Savior's genealogy in Matthew 1.[3]

Genesis 14:13

Many readers may not be aware of the semantic options for the Hebrew word for "brother." So the NIV includes a translator footnote on this verse to indicate that Hebrew *ʾāḥ* may not mean biological "brother" here but "relative" or even "ally." Participants in covenants or treaties between equals in the ancient Near East frequently called each other "brother," that is, treaty partner or ally.

Genesis 16:11, 14; 17:5, 19; 21:3

To help the English reader see and understand Hebrew wordplays, footnotes explain the meaning of certain names. For example, the footnote on Genesis 16:11 informs us that the name "Ishmael" means "God hears," enabling the reader to make the connection between the name and the verb "heard" in the verse. Similarly, the footnote on verse 14 indicates that Beer Lahai Roi means "well of the Living One who sees me," enabling the reader to see the association between the name in verse 14 and the expressions in verse 13: "You are the God who sees me" and "I have now seen the One who sees me." Again, the footnote on 17:5 explains that Abraham means "father of many," making it easier to connect the name with "father of many nations" in verses 4–5. Finally, the footnote on 17:19; 21:3 points out that the name "Isaac" means "he laughs," enabling the reader to make the connection between the name and the verb "laugh(ed)" in 17:17; 18:12–13, 15; 21:6. This kind of wordplay footnote occurs frequently in the NIV (see especially the footnotes on Mic. 1:10–15).

Genesis 34:10

Here the main text of the NIV translates the Hebrew verb *sāḥar* as "trade in." Yet the footnote allows for the alternative, "move about freely in." There is such strong evidence for the alternative (including the Akkadian and Aramaic cognates) that several commentators prefer it.[4] The NIV shows its balance by also allowing for this viable option.

Genesis 40:19, 22; 41:13

Lest readers misconstrue "hang you on a tree" (40:19) as meaning "suspend you from a tree with a rope around your neck until you die" (à la the Wild West), CBT provides the clarifying alternative rendering, "impale you on a pole." In a study note on Esther 2:23 the *NIVSB* comments not only on the same verb in that verse but also on the meaning of the passage in Genesis:

> Among the Persians this form of execution was impalement, as is confirmed in pictures and statues from the ancient Near East and in the comments of the Greek historian Herodotus (3.125, 129; 4.43). According to Herodotus (3.159) Darius I impaled 3,000 Babylonians when he took Babylon, an act that Darius himself

recorded in his Behistun (Bisitun) inscription. In Israelite and Canaanite practice, hanging was an exhibition of the corpse and not the means of execution itself (Dt 21:22–23; Jos 8:29; 10:26; 1 Sa 31:8–10; 2 Sa 4:12; 21:9–10). The execution of a chamberlain in the Joseph narrative also appears to have been by impalement (Ge 40:19). The sons of Haman were killed by the sword, and then their corpses were displayed in this way (9:5–14).[5]

Genesis 49:10

Here the NIV offers three options: (1) "until he comes to whom it belongs" (main text), (2) "until Shiloh comes" (first footnote alternative), and (3) "until he comes to whom tribute belongs" (second footnote alternative). Although difficult to translate, the verse has been traditionally understood as messianic. Probably it was initially and partially fulfilled in David, and ultimately and completely in Christ (including his second coming, from our perspective now).

If the first footnote alternative is correct, Shiloh would ultimately be a messianic title meaning something like "peace, rest, security" and presenting the Messiah as a peace-bringer. If the second footnote alternative is correct, it would anticipate a time when tribute would be brought to Judah's king (David/Messiah).

My preference is the main text, "until he comes to whom it [= 'scepter' or 'ruler's staff,' symbolizing kingdom or rule or kingship] belongs." The clause is repeated "almost verbatim in Eze 21:27 [MT 21:32] in a section where Zedekiah, the last king of Judah, is told to 'remove the crown' (Eze 21:26) from his head because dominion over Jerusalem will ultimately be given to the one 'to whom it rightfully belongs'"[6]—a clear allusion (at least to me) to Genesis 49:10. It is instructive to see the two clauses parallel to each other:

Genesis 49:10:   *ʿad kî-yābōʾ šîlōh*
Ezekiel 21:27/32:   *ʿad—bōʾ ʾăšer-lô*

The greater agreement by scholars on the understanding of the Ezekiel passage would seem to favor the same
sense in Genesis 49:10. In partial accord with BDB, *šîlōh*
should probably be repointed as *šellōh*.[7] This view is at
least partially, if not completely, supported by the Greek
Septuagint ("until the things stored up for him come"),
the Syriac Peshitta ("until he comes whose it is"), and the
Aramaic Targum Onkelos ("until the Messiah comes,
whose is the kingdom").

The following objections to such an understanding
are adduced by some: (1) One would expect *šellô* instead
of *šellōh* for the NIV sense. Normally that would be true,
but not in this context, where the same form of the third
masculine singular pronominal suffix occurs twice in
verse 11: *ʿîrōh* ("his donkey") and *sûtōh* ("his robes").
(2) One would expect *šellô hûʾ* instead of *šellōh*.[8] This
one mystifies me, for why must the masculine pronoun
be written twice? That would be redundant, and it is
often necessary to supply the verb "to be" in Hebrew, so
no copula is needed. I see nothing ungrammatical,
impossible, or even unlikely in such a construction. SS
1:6 *(šellî)* appears to be analogous. So I simply disagree
with such a subjective judgment. Moran's analysis of
Ezekiel 21:27/32 is even less convincing. There the NIV
has the most natural reading of the text.

(3) This view destroys the synonymous parallelism
with the following colon. Yet synthetic parallelism is
also very common in Hebrew poetry. (4) Such a use of
the relative particle *še* (and its variants) is said to be limited to late Hebrew. Yet Archer insists that it is used in
early Hebrew as well.[9] Its Akkadian counterpart *(ša)* is
attested even earlier. The Hebrew particle is used in the

song of Deborah (Judg. 5:7) and Job 19:29. (Most of its uses are in Ecclesiastes and Song of Songs.)

So I hold that the NIV main text is the most likely reading, the second footnote alternative is a close second, and the first footnote alternative is the least likely. In any event, the NIV maintains balance by providing alternative options.

Exodus 4:6

Although the NIV describes Moses' diseased hand as "leprous," the footnote (in the name of balance) points out that the skin disease referred to here (and elsewhere) may not be leprosy. A fuller explanation is given in one of my other books in Baker's NIV trilogy.[10]

Exodus 6:12

The NIV footnote indicates that the literal Hebrew for the clause "since I speak with faltering lips" is "since I am uncircumcised of lips." Since the literal rendering does not clearly communicate the sense, CBT interpreted the figure and translated its meaning with clarity. In Exodus 4:10 Moses had said that he was "slow of speech and tongue." Neither there nor here did he mean that he had a speech impediment (see Acts 7:22, "powerful in speech"). Rather, he felt that he was not eloquent or quick-witted enough to respond to the pharaoh. The literal expression used here is an excellent illustration of the fact that "literal" does not always equal "accurate," because at times it can be confusing and even misleading (inaccurate).[11]

Exodus 20:3

Should this commandment be rendered "You shall have no other gods *before* me" (main NIV text) or "You shall have no other gods *besides* me" (footnote alternative)? Of all the proposals for translating the Hebrew expression used here ("before," "besides," and others), "before" seems preferable because it is the most neutral, but the NIV allows the alternative as another option. Regardless of one's choice, the general sense is clear: The Lord wants his people to worship no other gods or idols in his presence. Nothing else is to compete with Israel's covenant Lord in their heart and life. He brooks no rivals.

Exodus 20:24

Here (and elsewhere) CBT chose "fellowship offerings" over the familiar "peace offerings," hence the explanatory footnote, "Traditionally *peace offerings*" (for balance). The *NIVSB* explains:

> Two basic ideas are included in this offering: peace and fellowship. The traditional translation is "peace offering," a name that comes from the Hebrew word for the offering, which in turn is related to the Hebrew word *shalom*, meaning "peace" or "wholeness." Thus the offering perhaps symbolized peace between God and man as well as the inward peace that resulted. The fellowship offering was the only sacrifice of which the offerer might eat a part. Fellowship was involved because the offerer, on the basis of the sacrifice, had fellowship with God and with the priest, who also ate part of the offering (7:14–15, 31–34).[12]

So the fellowship offering included a communal meal, thanksgiving, and fellowship. Fellowship or communion among the Lord, the priest, and the worshiper was established. Fellowship offerings included vow offerings, thank offerings, and freewill offerings (see chart on "Old Testament Sacrifices" at Lev. 4 in the *NIVSB*).

Exodus 21:6; 22:8–9, 28

Sometimes in legal literature it is difficult to determine whether Hebrew *ĕlōhîm* refers to "God" or his representatives, "judges" (either is possible—see the lexicons). Where CBT was somewhat uncertain, one was put in the main text and the alternative in a footnote (as in these verses).

Exodus 22:20

To help the reader more fully comprehend the particular Hebrew verb here rendered "destroyed," the NIV has a footnote explaining: "The Hebrew term refers to the irrevocable giving over of things or persons to the LORD, often by totally destroying them." As I have written elsewhere, "In the Old Testament, when defeated people and things were to be devoted to the Lord, it usually meant that everything perishable or flammable should be totally destroyed (cf. Josh 6–7), while gold and silver and other precious metals should be brought to the Lord's temple and used in his service."[13] This NIV footnote occurs frequently in the Old Testament.

Exodus 25:17

Why did the NIV call the lid of the ark of the covenant "an atonement cover" instead of "a mercy seat" (KJV and the footnote here)? The *NIVSB* study note here explains:

> *atonement*. Reconciliation, the divine act of grace whereby God draws to himself and makes "at one" with him those who were once alienated from him. In the OT, the shed blood of sacrificial offerings effected atonement . . . ; in the NT, the blood of Jesus, shed once for all time, does the same. . . . *atonement cover*. . . . That God's symbolic throne was capped with an atonement cover signified his great mercy toward his people.[14]

The study notes on Leviticus 16:2 and 17:11 are also helpful:

> *atonement cover.* . . . Blood sprinkled on the lid of the ark made atonement for Israel on the Day of Atonement (vv. 15–17). In the Septuagint (the Greek translation of the OT) the word for "atonement cover" is the same one used of Christ and translated "sacrifice of atonement" in Ro 3:25. . . .
>
> *blood . . . makes atonement.* Practically every sacrifice included the sprinkling or smearing of blood on the altar or within the tabernacle. . . , thus teaching that atonement involves the substitution of life for life. The blood of the OT sacrifice pointed forward to the blood of the Lamb of God, who obtained for his people "eternal redemption" (Heb 9:12). "Without the shedding of blood there is no forgiveness" (Heb 9:22).[15]

Exodus 28:20

The purpose of the footnote here is to inform the reader that the precise identification of some of the precious stones listed in verses 17–20 is uncertain. Indeed, the preface to the NIV has already alerted NIV users to the fact that "minerals, flora and fauna, architectural details, articles of clothing and jewelry, musical instruments and other articles cannot always be identified with precision."

Exodus 31:13

It is sometimes difficult to determine whether the form of the Hebrew verb used here *(qādaš)* should be translated as "make holy," "sanctify," or "set apart as holy." So between the main text and the two footnote alternatives, all three major possibilities are presented. In Scripture, to be "holy" is basically to be "separated" or "set apart to King Yahweh for his holy purposes and functions in his service and for his glory."[16]

Exodus 34:13

The translator footnote here enables the reader to understand that "Asherah poles" are wooden "symbols of the goddess Asherah." Elsewhere I have explained Asherah more fully:

> Asherah was a Canaanite fertility or mother goddess and consort of El (cf. Ugaritic ʾatrt, *Athirat*), and also the wooden cult object or "sacred pole" by which she was represented. Apparently, the plurals *Asherim* and *Asheroth* refer only to her images or cult objects. The contexts show that Asherah was a goddess (or an object representing her) who was worshiped along with Baal (Judg 3:7; 2 Kgs 23:6).[17]

Leviticus 16:8

The footnote helpfully defines the scapegoat as "the goat of removal; Hebrew *azazel.*" This goat was sent away alive bearing the sins of the nation (vv. 21–22), thus symbolizing the removal of the people's sin and guilt (cf. John 1:29).

Numbers 5:21

The final clause of this verse may be rendered either "when he [the LORD] causes your thigh to waste away and your abdomen to swell" (main text) or "when he causes you to have a miscarrying womb and barrenness" (footnote alternative).

The *NIVSB* explains:

> The figurative language here (and in vv. 22, 27) speaks of the loss of the capacity for childbearing (and, if pregnant, the miscarriage of the child). This is demonstrated by the determination of the fate of a woman wrongly charged (v. 28). For a woman in the ancient Near East

to be denied the ability to bear children was a personal loss of inestimable proportions. Since it was in the bearing of children that a woman's worth was realized in the ancient world, this was a grievous punishment indeed.[18]

Numbers 16:14

According to the footnote alternative, the Hebrew for "Will you gouge out the eyes of these men?" may also be rendered "Will you make slaves of these men?" or "Will you deceive these men?" Thus three options are presented. The first is a literal rendering of the original text. The other two represent figurative understandings of that literal language. Most commentators agree that the sense of the idiom is to "blind" in the sense of "deceive" or "mislead." Moses is accused of blinding the men to the true state of affairs so they will continue to follow his leadership.

Numbers 34:8

The footnote indicates that Lebo Hamath may be read as "the entrance to Hamath." The *NIVSB* explains why Lebo Hamath is preferable:

Lebo, however, probably does not mean "entrance," but should be identified with modern Lebweh, about 15 miles northeast of Baalbek and 20 miles southwest of Kadesh on the Orontes River, near Riblah. At one time Lebo must have served as a fortress guarding the southern route to Hamath. Perhaps the phrase should be translated "Lebo of Hamath." It is often referred to in Scripture as the northern limit of Israel (see v. 20; 48:1; Nu 13:21; 34:8; Jos 13:5; 1 Ki 8:65; 2 Ki 14:25; Am 6:14).[19]

Deuteronomy 3:11

In the footnote CBT recognizes a popular interpretation among other English Bible versions and commentaries, namely, that "bed" may refer to a sarcophagus (stone coffin). Millard, however, argues for the main text over the footnote alternative, pointing out that iron was in use this early as adornment, veneer, plating, and paneling. It would be analogous to the "iron" chariots in Joshua 17:16, where certain parts of the wooden chariots were apparently made of iron. In Millard's words:

> weapons and pieces of iron jewelry also survive from this period, and texts refer to more. . . . Even in the Middle Bronze Age (c. 1950–1550 B.C.), cuneiform tablets from Mari in Mesopotamia tell us of iron used in rings and bracelets.
>
> In southern Turkey an ivory box was unearthed from a level of the 18th century B.C. decorated with studs of gold, lapis lazuli and *iron*!
>
> From a Hittite text that can now be dated no later than the 16th century B.C., we find a reference to a "throne of iron" given as a gift by one ruler to another. . . . Doubtless the iron throne referred to here was wooden, embellished with iron.[20]

So King Og's bed may have been plated with iron—a rarity at the time that deserved mention in Deuteronomy.

Deuteronomy 6:4

Deuteronomy 6:4–9 is known as the *Shema*, Hebrew for the first word, "Hear" (see Mark 12:29–30). The Hebrew for "The LORD our God, the LORD is one" can be read in other ways as well (see the three footnote alternatives). Merrill favors the second alternative, "The LORD is our God, the LORD is one": "That is, the Divine Name should be construed as a nominative in each case and the terms 'our God' and 'one' as parallel predicate nominatives."[21] All the possible renderings either state explicitly or strongly imply the doctrine of monotheism, in addition to declaring that the LORD (Yahweh) is Israel's covenant God. "The consistent teaching of Moses and the prophets, as well as the psalmists and the wise men, admits of the Lord only as true deity."[22] Such a divine revelation is absolutely imperative in view of the multiplicity of other so-called gods worshiped in Canaan and elsewhere.

Deuteronomy 23:18

Here the difficulty is that a literal rendering of the Hebrew ("dog" instead of "male prostitute"; see NIV footnote) would be misleading and puzzling since most readers would not know how to understand the word "dog" in this context, where it is clearly figurative. The male prostitute is "disparingly described here as a 'dog.'"[23] The term is commonly associated with moral or spiritual impurity and is often used in a derogatory manner (cf. 1 Sam. 17:43; 24:14; 2 Sam. 9:8; 2 Kings 8:13; Matt. 7:6; Phil. 3:2; Rev. 22:15). To communicate the sense clearly, we provided what we believed to be the correct contextual nuance while furnishing the literal rendering in the footnote.

Deuteronomy 30:3

The Lord promises that when his chosen people return to him in obedience, he "will restore your fortunes," but the footnote allows for the alternative translation, "will bring you back from captivity." These two options appear quite frequently in the NIV, only sometimes in reverse order (with the latter rendering in the main text and the former in the footnote). Since the Hebrew can be translated either way, translators must decide on a case-by-case basis according to context. Where there is uncertainty, the alternative can be given in a footnote (as in the NIV).

Joshua 7:19

The NIV provides a footnote on Joshua's word to Achan ("give glory to the LORD"): "A solemn charge to tell the truth." So the sense is: "Give glory to the LORD by telling the truth" (see John 9:24). In the same context "confess to him" is presented as an alternative to "give him the praise." These contextual nuances in the two footnotes aid the reader's understanding of the main text and seem favored by Joshua's continuing address to Achan: "Tell me what you have done; do not hide it from me." These words are then followed by Achan's confession of sin (v. 20).

Judges 2:16; 4:4; 10:2

In Judges 2:16 the NIV, bowing to tradition, translated the Hebrew root *špṭ* as "judges" while offering "leaders" as the alternative in the "Or" footnote. In 4:4 and 10:2, however, CBT reversed the text and footnotes, with "leading" and "led" in the text and "judging" and "judged" in the footnotes. In the Mari letters the Akkadian equivalent of Hebrew *šōpēṭ* is *šāpiṭum*: "the *šāpiṭum* was appointed by the king . . . to act as a territorial governor, his activities including administration, the conduct of military campaigns, and the arbitration of domestic disputes."[24] This is a more accurate description of the functions of a *šōpēṭ* in Judges. Something like "leader" or "ruler" or "governor," then, would be closer than "judge" to the use of the term in the book of "Judges."

1 Samuel 3:13

According to the footnote, a *tiqqun sopherim* ("correction of/by the scribes"; see chapter 3: "The Old Testament") occurred here, changing "his sons blasphemed God" to "his sons made themselves contemptible." The former reading is supported by the LXX. Youngblood accepts it.[25] The penalty for such blasphemy was death (Lev. 24:13–16).

2 Samuel 8:18

Some readers may wonder why the NIV has "David's sons were royal advisers" when the Hebrew for "royal advisers" is the common word for "priests" (see the footnote alternative). The parallel passage in Chronicles has "David's sons were chief officials at the king's side" (1 Chron. 18:17), thus supporting the meaning "royal advisers" here instead of "priests." The *NIVSB* study note on 1 Chronicles 18:17 explains the situation:

> The earlier narrative at this point [2 Sam. 8:18] uses the Hebrew term ordinarily translated "priests". . . . The Chronicler has used a term for civil service instead of sacral service. Two approaches to this passage are ordinarily followed: 1. Some scholars see here an attempt by the Chronicler to keep the priesthood restricted to the Levitical line as part of his larger concern with legitimacy of cultic institutions in his own day. 2. Others argue that the Hebrew term used in 2 Sa 8:18 could earlier have had a broader meaning than "priest" and could be used of some other types of officials (cf. 2 Sa 20:26; 1 Ki 4:5). The Chronicler used an equivalent term, since by his day the Hebrew term for "priest" was restricted to cultic functionaries. The Septuagint, Targum, Old Latin and Josephus all translate the term in Samuel by some word other than "priest."

Personally I subscribe to the second approach above. Incidentally, almost all English Bibles use some phrase or word other than "priests" in the Samuel reference. For example, the KJV reads "chief rulers."

2 Samuel 22:30

The NIV main text reads "I can advance against a troop," while the footnote alternative offers "I can run through a barricade." The latter is a better parallel to the following "I can scale a wall." However, since a strong case can be made for either reading, the members of CBT again demonstrate their balanced approach by including both possibilities.

1 Kings 19:3

Was Elijah "afraid" (NIV text) when he "ran for his life," or did he "see" ("perceive" or "understand"; see NIV footnote)? Since it is possible to read the Hebrew text either way and a good case can be made for either, the NIV presents both options. The *NIVSB*, however, tips the scales in favor of the main text ("was afraid"):

> In spite of Elijah's great triumph in the trial on Mount Carmel and the dramatic demonstration that Elijah's God is the Lord of heaven and earth and the source of Israel's blessings, Jezebel is undaunted. Hers is no empty threat, and Ahab has shown that he is either unwilling or unable to restrain her. So Elijah knows that one of the main sources of Israel's present apostasy is still spewing out its poison and that his own life is in danger.[26]

2 Kings 3:11

Some readers might want to know why Elisha is described as one who "used to pour water on the hands of Elijah." So the NIV footnote explains the meaning: He "was Elijah's personal servant." Jones clarifies: "Elisha is designated as Elijah's servant. The custom of washing hands before and after eating is well attested; pouring water over the hands on such occasions was a gesture of respect shown by a servant to his master or by a host to his guest."[27]

2 Kings 8:10

The Hebrew text of Elisha's response here to Hazael's question as to whether Ben-Hadad (king of Aram) would recover from his illness (v. 9) may be read in two ways: (1) "Go and say to him 'You will certainly recover'; but the Lord has revealed to me that he will in fact die" (NIV main text); (2) "Go and say, 'You will certainly not recover,' for the Lord has revealed to me that he will in fact die" (footnote alternative). The *NIVSB* opts for the former, explaining, "This reading of the Hebrew text . . . is to be preferred (see v. 14) and understood as an assertion that Ben-Hadad's illness was not terminal."[28] So if he was going to die, it would not be because of the illness (v. 15).

2 Kings 15:5

Again the Hebrew here may be read in either one of two ways: (1) "he [Azariah/Uzziah] lived in a separate house" (NIV main text); (2) "he lived in a house where he was relieved of responsibility" (footnote alternative). In the parallel passage the *NIVSB* observes that "the same phrase in the Canaanite texts from Ugarit suggests a kind of quarantine or separation."[29] So while either rendering is possible and the NIV, for balance, provides both, the usage of the phrase in Ugaritic literature seems to support the reading in the NIV main text.

1 Chronicles 16:29

Here the NIV has "worship the Lord in the splendor of his holiness," but its "Or" footnote offers "worship the Lord with the splendor of holiness" as an alternative. The basic Hebrew for "in the splendor of his holiness/with the splendor of holiness" also occurs in 2 Chronicles 20:21; Psalms 29:2; 96:9; 110:3. Obviously the first option is descriptive of the Lord himself, while the second characterizes the worshiper. Which is correct? It is difficult to be certain, but the text (construction) and context of 2 Chronicles 20:21 seem to decide in favor of "in the splendor of his holiness."

Several commentators agree. Tate translates Psalm 96:9 as "bow down before Yahweh in (his) holy splendor."[30] Dillard renders 2 Chronicles 20:21 as "praise the splendor of his holiness."[31] Kidner says of Psalm 29:2 that "while it could be translated either way in all these places, the last of them [2 Chron. 20:21] tips the balance towards the 'literal' sense, understood as speaking of *God's* holiness rather than man's. Here, then, we should probably understand the line to mean 'Worship the Lord for the splendour of (his) holiness.'" He also has a footnote indicating that in 2 Chronicles 20:21 "the construction 'giving praise to the splendour of holiness' corresponds to 'give praise to the Lord,' two verses earlier. Hence NEB there: 'praise the splendour of his holiness.'"[32] Finally, Thompson comments on 1 Chronicles 16:29: "The probable meaning of the phrase is that the Lord's actions always display his holy splendor, for which he deserves holy worship." His footnote here points out that the "identical phrase is found in 2 Chr 20:21, but with the preposition *[lĕ]* 'for' rather than *[bĕ]* 'in.'" His comment on 2 Chronicles 20:21 is similar: "Jehoshaphat appointed men to sing to the Lord and to praise him for the splendor of his holiness as they went out at the head of the army."[33]

2 Chronicles 19:2

Some readers might not be familiar with the special uses of words like "love" and "hate" in certain contexts, so the NIV introduces them to one such probable usage in an "Or" footnote here, where "make alliances with those who hate the LORD" is presented as an alternative to "love those who hate the LORD." Selman notes, "*Love* and *hate* in this context are formal terms for actions within a covenant or treaty relationship rather than emotional feelings."[34] In a similar vein Thompson writes, "In some places in the Old Testament ['love'] carries a political rather than an emotional sense. No king of Israel who was loyal to the Lord should 'love,' that is, enter into a political and helping alliance, with one who 'hated' . . . the Lord."[35] Dillard adds, "There is ample background in ancient Near Eastern and biblical materials for translating *['āhab]* as 'make an alliance, be faithful to an alliance.'"[36]

Job 4:21

Sometimes it is difficult to determine where to end a quotation in the biblical text. Here is one such case, so CBT informs the reader: "Some interpreters end the quotation after verse 17" (see NIV footnote). Similar instances occur elsewhere (e.g., at John 3:21, 36; Gal. 2:21; see footnotes there).

Job 7:20

Even though most MSS of the MT read "I have become a burden to myself" at the end of this verse (see NIV footnote), CBT follows a few MSS of the MT, the LXX, and an ancient Hebrew scribal tradition in reading "Have I become a burden to you?" The *NIVSB* explains, "Ancient Hebrew scribes report that a change in the text had been made from 'you' to 'myself' because the reading 'you' involved too presumptuous a questioning of God's justice."[37]

Job 19:25–26

In this difficult and debated (but significant) passage, CBT (for balance) provides four alternative footnotes ("Or" readings). So if readers will avail themselves of these options, they will have all the most important and relevant data for interpretation (see also the *NIVSB* notes on 19:23–27 and the better exegetical commentaries on the passage).

Psalm 68:4

Readers may be curious as to why the NIV reads "extol him who rides on the clouds" here when the NASB has "Lift up a song for Him who rides through the deserts" (see the NIV footnote alternative). After all, there is quite a difference between riding "on the clouds" and riding "through the deserts." Elsewhere I have explained:

> This standing epithet of Baal ("rider of the clouds") may occur in Psalm 68:4, where the word "deserts" in Hebrew is probably a homonym of the word "clouds." If so, the verse should be rendered, "Sing to God; sing praises to His name. Lift up songs to (or Exalt or Prepare for) Him who rides on the clouds, whose name (or essence or revealed character) is the LORD . . . ; yes, rejoice before Him." The polemic would be that it is Yahweh, not Baal, who is the real rider of the clouds, i.e., Yahweh is the one who controls the rain and weather, and so fertility.[38]

The *NIVSB* adds: "An epithet of Baal found in Canaanite literature is used to make the point that the Lord (Yahweh, not Baal) is the exalted One who truly makes the storm cloud his chariot (see v. 33; 18:9; 104:3; Isa 19:1; Mt 26:64)."[39]

Proverbs 22:6

Which is correct—"Train a child in the way he should go" (NIV main text), "Start a child in the way he should go" (footnote alternative), or "Dedicate a child in the way he should go" (*NIVSB*, Prov. 22:6n.)? All are possible, so the NIV, with its balanced approach, allows for more than one rendering. In any event, Garrett summarizes the intent: "one should begin instructing a child in elementary principles of right and wrong as soon as possible."[40]

Song of Songs

To enable the reader to negotiate the changing speakers, the first footnote of the book (on the sectional heading *Beloved*) indicates:

> Primarily on the basis of the gender of the Hebrew pronouns used, male and female speakers are indicated in the margins by the captions *Lover* and *Beloved* respectively. The words of others are marked *Friends*. In some instances the divisions and their captions are debatable.

Song of Songs 8:6

The NIV main text reads at the end of the verse: "[Love] burns like blazing fire,/like a mighty flame." The footnote alternative ("Or") has a more literal rendering of the last colon: "like the very flame of the LORD." Why is it important to note this? "The Hebrew expression conveys the idea of a most intense flame, hinting that it has been kindled by the Lord."[41] Glickman paraphrases, "The fires of true love can never be quenched because the source of its flame is God himself."[42]

Isaiah 33:9

The Hebrew for "mourns" is *ʾābal,* which is now recognized as meaning "dry up" (NIV footnote alternative) in certain contexts.[43] In 24:4 the NIV so translated it. For that reason I would have reversed the text and footnote readings here.

Jeremiah 4:12

The difficulty here relates to "a wind too strong for that comes *from me*" versus "a wind too strong for that comes *at my command*" (footnote alternative). In this case the main text of the NIV has the more literal rendering. The only problem is the translation of the Hebrew preposition *l* as "from." But, as I have pointed out elsewhere,

> Prepositions have been a very fruitful field of Hebrew and Ugaritic comparative lexical study. Gordon observes: "The most interesting feature of Ugar. prepositions is the meaning 'from' for both *b* and *l*. The ambiguity of *b* and *l* is troublesome in reading Ugar.: *b* is either 'in(to), by, with' or 'from,' while *l* is 'to, for' or 'from.' However, even in the Old Testament, Hebrew *la-* and *ba-* sometimes mean 'from.'"
>
> A rather clear case of Hebrew [*l*] meaning "from" was encountered by the writer in translating Jeremiah 4:12.[44]

Jeremiah 25:26; 51:41

These verses refer to "Sheshach," but where is Sheshach? The NIV footnotes helpfully inform the reader that "*Sheshach* is a cryptogram for Babylon." The *NIVSB* further explains, "The cryptogram is formed by substituting the first consonant of the Hebrew alphabet for the last, the second for the next-to-last, etc. Its purpose is not fully understood, though in some cases the cryptogram itself bears a suitable meaning."[45] An example of a cryptogram with "a suitable meaning" is found in 51:1, where the NIV footnote indicates that "*Leb Kamai* is a cryptogram for Chaldea, that is, Babylonia." The *NIVSB* gives the meaning of Leb Kamai: "Lit. 'the heart of my attackers' (cf. Rev 17:5, where Babylon is called the mother of prostitutes and of the abominations of the earth)."[46]

Ezekiel 23:14

Reference is made here to Chaldeans, but who were they? The NIV footnote clarifies the situation to some extent: "Or *Babylonians.*" The *NIVSB* elaborates:

> The Chaldeans were the inhabitants of the southern regions of Mesopotamia who established the Neo-Babylonian empire (612–539 b.c.). Their origins are obscure. In the late seventh century b.c. the Chaldeans, led by Nebuchadnezzar's father Nabopolassar, overthrew the Assyrians.[47]

They are further described as a "people who were Bedouin until c. 1000 b.c., when they settled in southern Mesopotamia and later became the nucleus of Nebuchadnezzar's empire."[48]

Daniel 5:26–28

Here CBT assists the reader's understanding by pointing out (see the NIV footnotes) that *Mene* can mean "numbered" or *"mina"* (a unit of money), *Tekel* can mean "weighed" or *"shekel,"* and *Peres* (the singular of *Parsin*, v. 25) can mean "divided" or "Persia" or "a half *mina*" or "a half *shekel.*" This allows one to comprehend all the wordplays that are in view.

Daniel 6:28

One of the great historical perplexities of the Old Testament is the identity of Darius the Mede (Dan. 5:31; 6:1, 6, 9, 25, 28). While several solutions have been proposed, such as identifying him with Gubaru, the governor Cyrus put in charge of the newly conquered Babylonian territories, the simplest solution seems to be the reading suggested in the NIV footnote on 6:28: "So Daniel prospered during the reign of Darius, that is, the reign of Cyrus the Persian."[49] This would make "Darius the Mede" Cyrus's throne name in Babylon. It would also make this situation analogous to the one in 1 Chronicles 5:26, where Pul occurs as Tiglath-Pileser's throne name in Babylon (the Babylonians called him Pulu).

Amos 1:3

All the Hebrew has for "I will not turn back [my wrath]" is "I will not bring it back," which is why CBT put "my wrath" in brackets. To fully comprehend the ultimate meaning of this clause, it is not enough to know the meanings of isolated words. One must also become familiar with the concepts underlying the words, particularly idioms or modes of expression.

Specifically, one must comprehend the concept that actions have inevitable consequences unless there is divine intervention. In Amos 1:3, then, God is in effect assuring the Israelites that he will not intervene—destruction will come to Damascus as the inevitable consequence of their sins. The semantic development or extension is something like "I will not bring it back" = "I will not revoke punishment" or "I will not turn back (or call back) my wrath" (see Isa. 9:12; Jer. 23:20; Rom. 6:23; Gal. 6:7–8). Divine judgment will fall inexorably in this case. Finley basically concurs: "Each of the prophecies against the nations describes a judgment from the Lord, and it is this threat of which the Lord says, 'I will not turn it back.'"[50]

Amos 4:6

Since the literal Hebrew idiom "I gave you cleanness of teeth" might not be understood by many readers, CBT translated it "I gave you empty stomachs" and put the literal rendering in the footnote. Again the development is

"I gave you cleanness of teeth" = "I gave you famine" or "I gave you empty stomachs" (with no food to make your teeth dirty, hence "cleanness of teeth"). "The teeth are clean, of course, when there is nothing to eat."[51] The parallel ("lack of bread") shows that the sending of famine is the intended sense.

Micah 5:2

Although I have already dealt with this verse,[52] I list it again to call attention to my recent, more complete treatment.[53]

Habakkuk 2:4

The NIV main text reads "the righteous will live by his faith," while the footnote alternative has "the righteous will live by his faithfulness." Too much has been written about the alleged difference between faith and faithfulness. Distinctions can be made, but far too often the lines have been drawn too sharply. A person of faith will be faithful, and one who is faithful will possess faith. Long ago, Lightfoot correctly wrote: "The Hebrew [*'ĕmûnâ*], the Greek [*pistis*], the Latin 'fides,' and the English 'faith,' hover between two meanings; *trustfulness* [= faith], the frame of mind which relies on another; and *trustworthiness* [= faithfulness], the frame of mind which can be relied upon. . . . the two senses will at times be so blended together that they can only be separated by some arbitrary distinction."[54]

In view of such studies as those cited in the previous footnote, I do not share the narrow view that *'ĕmûnâ* always and only means "faithfulness." Although it most often means "faithfulness, reliability, dependability, trustworthiness," occasionally it comes closer to the notion of "faith, belief, trust." In the context of Habakkuk 2:4, it seems best to let the primary emphasis fall on the concept of "faith." That is to say, in the light of God's revelation as to how and when he is working, Habakkuk is to wait patiently and live by faith—trusting in the sovereign God. He is to persevere in the related concepts of faith and faithfulness.

Zechariah 12:10

Two footnote alternatives are offered for this verse. The first would take "a spirit" in the sense of the Holy Spirit, hence "the Spirit" (cf. "the Spirit of grace" in Heb. 10:29). In the context of the book itself (4:6; 7:12) as well as of similar passages elsewhere (Isa. 32:15; 44:3; 59:21; Ezek. 36:27; 39:29; Joel 2:28–29), this seems preferable:

> In anthropomorphic language the Lord promises an effusion of his Spirit on his covenant people. The imagery is doubtless that of water as an emblem of the Holy Spirit. The recipients are the royal leaders and people of Jerusalem, representative of the inhabitants of the whole land. The content of the effusion is . . . "the Spirit which conveys grace and calls forth supplications" (Perowne, pp. 132–33). . . . Because of the convicting work of God's Spirit, Israel will turn to the Messiah with mourning.[55]

The second footnote alternative ("look to" instead of "look on") is probably also to be preferred: "The most common meaning of the Hebrew preposition translated 'on' is 'to'. . . , and there is no good contextual reason to depart from it here. The emphasis, then, is not on looking 'on' (or 'at') the Messiah literally but on looking 'to' the Messiah in faith (cf. Num. 21:9; Isa. 45:22; John 3:14–15)."[56]

Matthew 1:17

CBT wanted to alert the reader to the fact that "Christ" in the New Testament is often to be understood in the

Old Testament sense of "Messiah," hence the footnote alternative: "Or *Messiah*. 'The Christ' (Greek) and 'the Messiah' (Hebrew) both mean 'the Anointed One.'"

Matthew 1:21

To help readers relate the name "Jesus" to the verb "save," the NIV footnote explains, "*Jesus* is the Greek form of *Joshua*, which means *the LORD saves*."

Matthew 5:22

To help the reader understand something of the function of Raca in the sentence, the footnote clarifies that it is an "Aramaic term of contempt." It may "be related to the Aramaic word for 'empty' and mean 'Empty-head!'"[57]

Matthew 6:27

Which is correct—"add a single hour to his life" (main text) or "add a single cubit to his height" (footnote alternative)? Since a good case can be made for both, the NIV allows for either, although obviously preferring the main text.

Matthew 9:10–11

"Sinners" is in quotation marks to indicate that the word is used in a way that is different from its ordinary use. In the New Testament the term was used not only of notoriously evil people but also of those who did not follow the Mosaic Law as interpreted by the teachers of the Law. It "was commonly used of tax collectors, adulterers, robbers and the like."[58]

Matthew 23:5

What are phylacteries? The footnote describes them as "boxes containing Scripture verses, worn on forehead and arm." They contained Exodus 13:1–10, 11–16; Deuteronomy 6:4–9; 11:13–21. The *NIVSB* note on Exodus 13:9 elaborates:

> A literal reading of this verse has led to the practice of writing the texts of vv. 1–10, vv. 11–16, Dt 6:4–9 and Dt 11:13–21 on separate strips of parchment and placing them in two small leather boxes, which the observant Jew straps on his forehead and left arm before his morning prayers. The boxes are called "phylacteries" (Mt 23:5). This practice seems to have originated after the exile to Babylon.

Luke 2:14

> "Glory to God in the highest,
> and on earth peace to men
> on whom his favor rests."

What happened to "peace, good will toward men" (KJV)? Yamauchi explains:

> Although the translation of the King James Version is accurate, the Greek text it used is not. That Greek text, known as the Textus Receptus, was based on the first printed Greek New Testament issued by Erasmus in 1516. Working in haste, Erasmus was able to use but seven inferior and late manuscripts available at Basel. Today, on the basis of hundreds of earlier manuscripts, we now have a Greek text that is far more accurate. In the vast majority of cases, the improvements are minor and make little difference, but in some cases, the sense is dramatically altered. One of those cases is Luke 2:14, where the difference of a single letter changes entirely the meaning of the text.
>
> The Textus Receptus has *en anthrōpois eudokia*, whereas the best manuscripts read *en anthrōpois eudokias*. In the first case, the word *eudokia* (good will)

may be taken as a parallel to peace as a subject. In the second case, *eudokias* qualifies *anthrōpois* (men or people). That is to say, peace was not promised to all men in general, but only to "men of [God's] good will."

The Greek parallels a Hebrew phrase found in the Dead Sea Scrolls, *bnei retsono,* "sons of His [i.e., God's] will." Hence, the RSV renders the line "and on earth peace among men with whom he is pleased," and the NIV has "and on earth peace to men on whom his favor rests."[59]

Luke 17:21

What did Jesus mean when he said that "the kingdom of God is within you"? This verse illustrates the careful skill and sound judgment required in translating the Bible. Many Bible translators (including this one) believe that the word "within" is better rendered "among" (as in the NIV footnote alternative). The *NIVSB* comments on "the kingdom of God is within you":

> Probably indicating that the kingdom is spiritual and internal (Mt 23:26), rather than physical and external (cf. Jn 18:36). But see NIV text note (cf. 19:11; 21:7; Ac 1:6), meaning that the kingdom is present in the person of its king, Jesus (see also note on 4:43). However, the immediate context (v. 20) may favor the former interpretation, namely, that the kingdom is spiritual and so not visible. If this is the correct view, the pronoun "you" in the phrase "within you" is to be taken in a general sense rather than as referring to the unbelieving Pharisees personally. The kingdom certainly was not within them.[60]

1 Corinthians 6:12

Why the quotation marks? "Paul is probably quoting some in the Corinthian congregation who boasted that they had a right to do anything they pleased. The apostle counters by observing that such 'freedom' of action may not benefit the Christian." Similarly in verse 13, "Paul quotes some Corinthians again who were claiming that as the physical acts of eating and digesting food have no bearing on one's inner spiritual life, so the physical act of promiscuous sexual activity does not affect one's spiritual life."[61] Paul counters this line of reasoning in the rest of verse 13. The use of quotation marks in these instances makes it clear to the reader that Paul is quoting and then responding to slogans hurled at him by the Corinthians.

2 Thessalonians 2:15

If the Greek word *paradosis* means "tradition" (see NIV footnote alternative), why wasn't the plural translated "traditions" here instead of "teachings"? After all, *paradosis* was rendered "tradition" in Matthew 15:2. When *paradosis* was used in a positive way to refer to the passing on of apostolic teachings, we did not want the reader to think of "the tradition of the elders" (Matt. 15:2) or of traditions in general, but of apostolic teachings in particular. So when we believed that reference was to the latter, we usually rendered the term as "teachings" to make that meaning clear to readers. All words must be contextually nuanced. By providing a footnote alternative ("tradition" or "traditions"), we are telling the reader that in those instances we believe that what is being "handed down" is the apostolic "teachings."

1 Timothy 1:9

It is sometimes difficult to determine whether "law" refers to law in general or the Mosaic Law in particular. Here the main text has the more general reference, while the footnote alternative provides the more particular reading. The commentaries are divided on the issue, so the NIV allows for either understanding.

Philemon 10

Here the NIV explanatory note (*"Onesimus* means *useful"*) helps the reader see the wordplay between the meaning of the name and "useful" in verse 11 (similarly with "benefit" in v. 20).

Hebrews 3:11

"They shall never enter my rest" is another illustration of why we cannot always translate literally. The Greek says literally "If they shall enter my rest." But the Greek text here reproduces a Hebrew idiom in an oath formula, in which *ʾim* ("if") is used for emphatic negation (= "certainly not"—NIV "never").[62]

Hebrews 7:25

Is Jesus able to save "completely" (NIV main text) or "forever" (footnote alternative)? Perhaps both ideas are included here: "Jesus is a perfect high priest forever; so he is able to save completely and for all time."[63]

Revelation 1:20

This will have to suffice as the last of the examples selected to demonstrate that CBT followed a balanced approach in handling difficulties. Here the problem has to do with the semantic nuance of Greek *angeloi* in this context. The footnote alternative helps by reminding the reader of the root idea of "angels" namely, "messengers." But who are they? At least four major options have been presented: (1) heavenly messengers (angels who are guardians of the seven churches), (2) personifications of the prevailing spirit of each church, (3) earthly messengers (the principal human ministers or leaders of the churches), and (4) human representatives of the churches but not necessarily the sole or chief leaders. Thomas favors the latter.[64]

So a good translation will use balance in handling difficult passages.[65]

6

A Balanced Selection of Available Resources

If a Bible translation is to be truly good enough to be widely used by the universal church, it must have a wide range of balanced works that are keyed to it and that support its text. Study tools, reference works, commentaries, and other resources will be based on it. The NIV, for example, has an unusual abundance of supporting resources. The following is only a partial and highly selective list of such works by category.

1. Study Bibles

The NIV Study Bible
Disciples Study Bible
Life Application Bible
The Student Bible
The Ryrie Study Bible
Thompson Chain-Reference Bible
The International Inductive Study Bible
The Teen Study Bible
The New Scofield Study Bible
The Quest Study Bible
The Living Insights Study Bible
The Concordia Self-Study Bible
The NIV Thematic Reference Bible

2. Concordances, Interlinears, and Triglot

NIV Exhaustive Concordance
NIV Hebrew-English Concordance
NIV Greek-English Concordance
Interlinear NIV Hebrew-English Old Testament
NIV Interlinear Greek-English New Testament
NIV Triglot Old Testament (Hebrew-Greek-NIV)

3. Commentaries

One-Volume and Two-Volume Commentaries:

New Bible Commentary 21st Century Edition (1 vol.)
International Bible Commentary (1 vol.)
Evangelical Commentary on the Bible (1 vol.)
Zondervan NIV Bible Commentary (2 vols.)
Bible Knowledge Commentary (2 vols.)

Multivolume Sets:

Expositor's Bible Commentary
New American Commentary
New International Biblical Commentary
NIV Application Commentary
New Testament Commentary

4. Dictionaries and Encyclopedias

New International Dictionary of the Bible
Zondervan Pictorial Encyclopedia of the Bible
New International Dictionary of Old Testament Theology and Exegesis

New International Dictionary of New Testament Theology

5. Topical Bibles and Atlas

Zondervan NIV Nave's Topical Bible
Topical Analysis of the Bible
Zondervan NIV Atlas of the Bible

6. The NIV on Computer

The NIV Study Bible Complete Library
Zondervan New International Version Bible
Bible Source
MacBible
Thompson Chain HyperBible
BibleMaster
CompuBible
Gramcord
Logos Bible Software
QuickVerse
WordSearch
Bible Companion
OnLine Bible USA
OnLine Bible Macintosh
PC Study Bible

The above works involve over a dozen different publishers. With such a wealth of supporting resources (and still more planned for the future), it is not surprising that over thirty denominations either sanction or extensively use the NIV.

So a good translation will have a wide range of balanced works available to support its text.

7

Balance Is the Key

As we indicated at the outset, if the church is to really hear God's Word with authority, accuracy, and clarity, it must use a good translation. Such a translation will exhibit a pleasing balance in its committee approach and membership, in its textual basis, in its translation philosophy, in handling difficult passages, and in the selection of study tools, reference works, commentaries, and other resources that are based on it. Among other things, we have attempted to demonstrate that the NIV is one translation that meets these criteria.

Others agree. For instance, Purkiser says:

> A most recent translation that offers great promise is the *New International Version.* While not sectarian in any sense, the scholars who worked on the NIV are all dedicated, evangelical Christians. I have watched their work from the beginning, and believe they have given us the best translation into contemporary English yet to be made.[1]

And Burdick has written:

> In conclusion, we have been saying that a good translation is neither too much nor too little. It is neither too slavish a reproduction of the Greek [and Hebrew], nor is it too free in its handling of the original. It is neither too modern and casual, nor is it too stilted and formal.

It is not too much like the KJV, nor does it depart too far from the time-honored beauty and dignity of that seventeenth-century classic. In short, the best translation is one that has avoided the extremes and has achieved instead the balance that will appeal to the most people for the longest period of time.[2]

Ewert declares, "The NIV is undoubtedly a monument to evangelical scholarship and one of the best all-purpose Bibles available to English-speaking Christians."[3] Kucharsky likewise claims, "But after all the comparisons are made, the NIV must be recognized as [a translation] of exceptional quality. It represents perhaps the finest work of evangelical scholarship in this century."[4]

God's Word is too important to be hidden in language that may be confusing to today's reader. While some versions have held on to the style and vocabulary of the Elizabethan English of 1611, the NIV was written specifically to speak to modern readers in a contemporary English that is easy to read and understand.

Does all this mean that the NIV is perfect? No, it does not. In fact, no translation is perfect, for they are all made by imperfect people. Nonetheless, as I have written elsewhere, "one advantage of using the NIV is that, in spite of its imperfections, most expositors will likely experience the pleasant surprise that they are devoting less time to correcting and clarifying the text than would be the case if they were using some other English Bible."[5]

The need for "new and improved" translations will always exist. Lewis explains:

A translation starts to become outdated from the moment it is completed. Information from new manuscript materials, new insights into the languages in which the Bible was first written, and new data concerning biblical history need to be communicated to the reader. Changing ideas about translations and changes in the English language itself all outdate a version, thus preparing the way for the process to be started all over again. . . .

I have been impressed with the number of times that I thought I had found an error in the work of a translation group, but additional investigation made it clear that the beam was in my own eye, not in the translator's.[6]

We can all learn a valuable lesson from the prologue of the apocryphal work Ecclesiasticus, also known as the Wisdom of Jesus son of Sirach (I have taken the liberty of making two editorial changes in brackets to make an application to the NIV): "You are invited therefore to read [the NIV translation] with goodwill and attention, and to be indulgent in cases where, despite our diligent labor in translating, we may seem to have rendered some phrases imperfectly. For what was originally expressed in Hebrew [and Greek] does not have exactly the same sense when translated into another language" (NRSV).

Silva puts it like this:

> When the editor of *New Horizons* asked me if I would be interested in writing a response to criticisms of the NIV, I hesitated briefly. After all, I was not involved in the translating of the NIV. Moreover, I think the NIV is far from perfect.
>
> During the past few years, I have been involved in the production of an "NIV-like" translation of the Bible into Spanish. This work, which involves very close comparison of the NIV with the original, has alerted me to numerous renderings that appear unsatisfying, problematic, or even plain wrong. In other words, my own list of objections is probably much longer than that of most outspoken critics of the NIV.
>
> So why would I then agree to write this article? Simply because my list of objections to *other* versions would be even longer [emphasis his]. This is not to say that all available English translations are bad. Quite the con-

trary! We are richly blessed by a wide variety of versions, almost all of which—when compared with good translations of other literature—have to be regarded as clear and accurate, but never perfect. . . .

Different versions have different strengths. The (N)KJV is most majestic (even when the original is not!). The Good News Bible communicates most simply. The NASB is most useful for detailed study. And so on. But among available English translations of the Bible, the NIV, whatever faults it may have, sports the best combination of reliability, naturalness of style, and respect for the religious tradition to which evangelical and Reformed Christians belong. It may be used with confidence and profit.[7]

Fee and Stuart add their evaluation: "We would venture to suggest that the NIV is as good a translation as you will get."[8]

Whether one chooses the NIV or one of the other good translations, I believe the time has come for every denomination and every church to adopt one version as its official Bible and use it for everything—pew Bible, preaching, public reading of Scripture, Sunday school, Scripture memorization, and so on. This is not to say that in the early elementary grades, and so at lower reading levels, one should not use simple, easy-reading versions like the NIrV. Indeed the NIrV nicely prepares the way for the transition to the NIV (on which it is based). Bastian agrees with the basic premise I have stated here:

> The time has come for each congregation to center its life on one version . . . The plethora of Bible translations into English—approximately 70 of all or parts of the Bible in this century—may only have nourished a spirit of novelty among us, making us samplers rather than searchers.

If a church is to use the Bible systematically, it must center its whole life—preaching, teaching, family and personal devotions—upon one major version, because repetition aids learning. Moreover, a congregation working from a Bible common to both pulpit and pew receives the message by the eye gate as well as the ear gate, providing another aid to understanding. . . .

You may not agree, or you may argue that the choice is much wider than I allow [he recommends the NIV over the RSV]. Either way, I hope you agree that the time has come for congregations to form their life around one major version until its great words fix themselves in the minds and hearts of worshipers of all ages.[9]

The most important thing is for a church to begin really hearing God's Word through whatever good translation it selects. And may we all hear it in the frequent Hebrew and Greek sense of "hear": "listen, understand, and obey with an appropriate response."

A most fitting conclusion to this book (but see Appendix) comes from Metzger:

Translating the Bible is a never-ending task. As long as English remains a living language it will continue to change, and therefore new renderings of the Scriptures will be needed. Furthermore, as other, and perhaps still more, ancient manuscripts come to light, scholars will need to evaluate the history of the scribal transmission of the original texts. And, let it be said finally, alongside such developments in translating the Bible there always remains the duty of all believers to translate the teaching of Holy Writ into their personal lives.[10]

Appendix

Answers to
Miscellaneous Questions

1. Q: Out of all the books, pamphlets, and booklets I have read about the NIV, there is really none that provides a personal touch about the translators themselves. They give me facts, information, and other historical data, but few personal anecdotes. Why hasn't such a book been written?
A: Actually such a book already exists. It was written by Burton L. Goddard (a CBT member), is entitled *The NIV Story: The Inside Story of the New International Version,* and was published by Vantage Press in 1989 in New York City. In the words of the book jacket, "The author, who from the early beginnings was a participant in creating the New International Version, provides us with a compelling history of the task in all of its drama and complexity."

2. Q: Was there really a need for a new Bible translation like the NIV?
A: Our position on this mattter and other related issues is essentially the same as that of the KJV translators. The following lengthy quotation is from "The Translators to the Reader" at the front of the 1611 KJV:

Without translation into the vulgar tongue, the unlearned are but like children at Jacob's well (which was deep) without a bucket or something to draw with. . . . Many men's mouths have been open a good while (and yet are not stopped) with speeches about the Translation so long in hand . . . and ask what may be the reason, what the necessity of the employment: Has the Church been deceived, say they, all this while? . . . Was their Translation good before? Why do they now mend it?. . . . We affirm and avow that the very meanest translation of the Bible in English . . . containeth the word of God, nay, is the word of God. . . . Neither did we disdain to revise that which we had done, and to bring back to the anvil that which we had hammered. . . . Some peradventure would have no variety of senses to be set in the margin, lest the authority of the Scriptures for deciding of controversies by that show of uncertainty should somewhat be shaken. But we hold their judgment not to be so sound in this point.

3. Q: Has anyone responded to Robert P. Martin's criticism of the NIV in his book, *Accuracy of Translation and the NIV* (Carlisle, Pa.: Banner of Truth, 1989)?
   A: Martin argues for the inaccuracy of the NIV on seven grounds. Bob Sheehan refutes five and partially agrees with two in his article, "Criticism of the NIV" (a review of Martin's book), *Reformation Today* 114 (March–April 1990): 15–19. In addition, I have responded to several points in *The Accuracy of the NIV,* particularly on pp. 12–17, 56, 85–86.

4. Q: Hasn't the KJV's superiority to the NIV been demonstrated by its more widespread and favorable reception initially?
   A: I will let Ewert answer this one:

Critics accused the [KJV] translators of blasphemy and modernism, and called them "damnable corrupters." The AV was denounced as being unfaithful to the original, and one London clergyman thought it denied the deity of Jesus Christ. . . .

The Dissenters who fled to America took the Geneva Bible with them, since in their view, the AV reminded them too much of the divine right of kings. Attacks on the AV continued almost to the end of the seventeenth century, but eventually this version won out over all others.[1]

5. Q: What is the significance of "New" and "International" in the title?

A: It is "New" because it is not a revision of a previously existing version. Rather, it is a fresh translation directly from the Hebrew, Aramaic, and Greek texts. It is "International" for at least two reasons: (1) We had an international team of translators, representing all the major English-speaking countries of the world; (2) we attempted to use international English and so avoid as many overt Americanisms and Anglicisms as possible.

6. Q: One Christian leader told me that people do not become Christians through reading modern translations like the NIV, but that they do become Christians by reading the KJV. Is that true?

A: No, it is not. In my files I have several letters that disprove that claim. Here is one dated September 1, 1994, from Madison, Wisconsin: "I was led to my Lord Jesus Christ through my NIV, which was a gift from my spiritual mother and physical mother-in-law. I was further discipled and continue to grow in my knowledge and faith of God and his Word through the NIV."

7. Q: Why do you not capitalize pronouns referring to deity?

A: First, the inspired Hebrew, Aramaic, and Greek texts make no such distinction in pronouns, whether referring to the Trinity or to humans. Second, we are following time-honored tradition in English Bible translation history. For example, the KJV did not capitalize pronouns referring to the Godhead. In fact, out of over a hundred English translations of the Bible, I am aware of only two that capitalize such pronouns: the NASB and the NKJV. Third, it is not really a matter of respect or reverence for God, because respect for God is ultimately and primarily a matter of the heart. And the NIV translators have just as much respect and reverence for the Lord as anyone.

8. Q: Do you believe that the NIV will be one of the few enduring English versions and will continue to be the best-selling Bible in the world?
A: I have already been quoted on this issue and am not willing to go beyond this statement: "the NIV will stand the test of time and will be one of the few current translations that will endure. I expect it will eventually enjoy the most widespread use among evangelicals, evangelical churches, and a significant number of nonevangelicals."[2]

Bright, however, explains why he believes that there will never be a once-for-all translation (without updates) or one that will be universally acceptable:

To translate anything from one language into another is, as anyone who has ever attempted it knows, a ticklish business. . . . The translator faces a twofold task, and he cannot for so much as a sentence forget it if he hopes to succeed in discharging his obligation. He must catch the precise meaning of the words in their original language, and then bring that meaning into the recipient, or translation, language with equal precision; and he must do this in such a way that the literary quality of the original is preserved and, as far as possible, its idiom recreated. In other words, he must see to it that what was *communicated* to readers of the original language . . . is also communicated to readers of the recipient language. . . . The thing simply cannot be done to perfection. . . . it is safe to say that no translation has ever been made, or ever will be, that can claim to be 100 per cent successful. This, of course, goes far to explain why there can never be a once-for-all translation of the Bible into English, or even one that will be universally acceptable at a given time and place.[3]

9. Q: What general principles or guidelines did you follow in translating the NIV?
A: The following are found in our unpublished "Translators' Manual" (dated 11/29/68):

(1) At every point the translation shall be faithful to the Word of God as represented by the most accurate text of the original languages of Scripture.
(2) The work shall not be a revision of another version but a fresh translation from the Hebrew, Aramaic, and Greek.
(3) The translation shall reflect clearly the unity and harmony of the Spirit-inspired writings.
(4) The aim shall be to make the translation represent as clearly as possible only what the original says, and not to inject additional elements by unwarranted paraphrasing.
(5) The translation shall be designed to communicate the truth of God's revelation as effectively as possible to English readers in the language of the people. In this respect the Committee's goal is that of doing for our own times what the King James Version did for its day.

(6) Every effort shall be made to achieve good English style.

(7) The finished product shall be suitable for use in public worship, in the study of the Word, and in devotional reading.

(8) All those engaged by the Committee as translators or editors shall be required to affirm the following article of faith (see chapter 2).

The following additional statements appear later in this same document:

(1) Translators should keep the principles of the translation constantly in mind and strive for accuracy, clarity, and force of expression.

(2) Translators should do their work originally from the original language, but before the completion of their work representative translations and commentaries shall be consulted.

(3) Certain notes of text variation, alternative translation, cross-reference, or explanation will be put in the margin.

(4) The purpose of the project is not to prepare a word-for-word translation nor yet a paraphrase.

(5) Read the passages as a whole and aloud to check for euphony and suitability for public reading.

10. Q: Which translation is really inspired?
    A: Gromacki answers this question in his fifth statement below. However, all seven of his declarations on "Explanation of Inspiration" are worthy of being listed, so here they are:
    (1) Only the Bible is inspired of God.
    (2) The Bible is the inspired truth.
    (3) The Bible is inspired equally throughout all sixty-six books.

(4) The Bible is inspired down to the very words the authors used.

(5) Technically speaking, the Bible is inspired in only the original writings that the Spirit-directed authors wrote.

Practically speaking, it is still possible to say that translations such as the KJV, NASB, and NIV also are inspired to the extent that they faithfully represent the content of the original writings. This distinction between the original writings and subsequent copies, versions, and translations must be seen and understood.

(6) The Bible is inerrant and infallible in all matters it addresses.

(7) The Bible is the supreme, authoritative basis of faith and practice.

In addition, he has four helpful observations on "Attitudes Toward Translations":

(1) We should be thankful that we can use these English versions for our personal edification.

(2) We should not permit the usage of a particular version to become the basis of personal and ecclesiastical fellowship.

(3) We can have confidence that the major English versions protect and propagate the evangelical Christian faith. (He recommends the KJV, NKJV, NIV, and NASB.)

(4) We should read prayerfully and carefully.[4]

Answers to additional questions may be found in the other two books in Baker's NIV trilogy *(The Making of the NIV* and *The Accuracy of the NIV),* as well as in the booklet, "Questions & Answers about the NIV" (available from IBS in Colorado Springs, Colo.).

Notes

Chapter 1: *Balance Is the Key*

1. The source of the KJV sales figure is *The Sunday Post* of Glasgow, Scotland (March 26, 1995), 38.

2. K.L. Barker, "Hearing God's Word Through a Good Translation," in *Reading and Hearing the Word: From Text to Sermon*, ed. A.C. Leder (Grand Rapids: CRC Publications, 1998), 17–31. Appreciation is hereby expressed to the publisher for permission to use that material.

Chapter 2: *A Balanced Committee Approach*

1. "The Story of the New International Version" (Colorado Springs, Colo.: International Bible Society, 1978), 8.

2. Quoted in *A Bible for Today and Tomorrow* (London: Hodder & Stoughton, 1989), 39.

Chapter 3: *A Balanced Textual Basis*

1. B.S. Childs, *Introduction to the Old Testament as Scripture* (Philadelphia: Fortress, 1979), 97.

2. J.T. Barrera, *The Jewish Bible and the Christian Bible*, trans. W.G.E. Watson (Grand Rapids: Eerdmans, 1998), 378.

3. B.M. Metzger, "Handing Down the Bible Through the Ages: The Role of Scribe and Translator," *RR* 43 (Spring 1990): 162.

4. E. Tov, *The Text-Critical Use of the Septuagint in Biblical Research* (Jerusalem: Simon, 1981), 287.

5. B.K. Waltke, "The Textual Criticism of the Old Testament," in *Biblical Criticism: Historical, Literary and Textual* by R.K. Harrison et al. (Grand Rapids: Zondervan, 1978), 77–78; cf. also E. Wurthwein, *The Text of the Old Testament*, trans. E.F. Rhodes (Grand Rapids: Eerdmans, 1979), 116–17. For the "varied history" of the text of the Hebrew Bible referred to above, see Waltke, ibid., 47–77; F.M. Cross, Jr., "The Contribution of the Qumrân Discoveries to the Study of the Biblical Text," in *Qumran and the History of the Biblical Text*, ed. F.M. Cross, Jr., and S. Talmon (Cambridge: Harvard, 1975), 290–92 (a summary).

6. K.L. Barker, "Zechariah," in *EBC*, ed. F.E. Gaebelein (Grand Rapids: Zondervan, 1985), 7:635 (n. on 5:6), 639, 692 (n. on 14:5).

7. W. Eichrodt, *Theology of the Old Testament*, trans. J.A. Baker (Philadelphia: Westminster, 1967), 2:343 n. 1.

8. J.G. Baldwin, *Haggai, Zechariah, Malachi*, TOTC (Downers Grove, Ill.: InterVarsity, 1972), 128.

9. H.L. Ginsberg, "The North-Canaanite Myth of Anath and Aqhat," *BASOR* 98 (April 1945): 21; cf. also Ginsberg, "Ugaritic Studies and the Bible," *BA* 8 (May 1945): 57–58.

10. W.F. Albright, "A New Hebrew Word for 'Glaze' in Proverbs 26:23," *BASOR* 98 (April 1945): 24.

11. Ibid.

12. The translation is mine; the text is 2Aqhat 6:36–38 and may be found in C.H. Gordon, *Ugaritic Textbook* (Rome: Pontifical Biblical Institute, 1965), 249.

13. K.A. Kitchen, *Ancient Orient and Old Testament* (Chicago: InterVarsity, 1966), 163; on the enclitic *mêm* he mentions, cf. H.D. Hummel, "Enclitic *Mem* in Early Northwest Semitic, Especially Hebrew," *JBL* 76 (1957): 85–107.

14. See further K.L. Barker, "The Value of Ugaritic for Old Testament Studies," *Bib. Sac.* 133 (April 1976): 128–29; A.P. Ross, "Proverbs," in *EBC*, 5:1092–93; D.A. Garrett, *Proverbs, Ecclesiastes, Song of Songs*, NAC (Nashville: Broadman & Holman, 1993), 215; R.L. Alden, *Proverbs* (Grand Rapids: Baker, 1983), 189.

15. W.F. Albright, "A New Hebrew Word for 'Glaze' in Proverbs 26:23," 24.

16. See D.A. Hubbard, *Joel and Amos*, TOTC (Downers Grove, Ill.: InterVarsity, 1989), 198. For further examples of OT textual criticism at work, see K.L. Barker, *The Accuracy of the NIV* (Grand Rapids: Baker, 1996), 23 (Gen. 4:8), 28 (2 Sam. 21:19), 29 (1 Kings 22:38), 36 (Ps. 100:3), 44 (Isa. 53:11), 46 (Ezek. 34:16), 47 (Ezek. 45:1); B.K. Waltke, "The *New International Version* and Its Textual Principles in the Book of Psalms," *JETS* 32 (March 1989): 17–26; Waltke, "Psalms 2 and 4," in *The Making of the NIV*, ed. K.L. Barker (Grand Rapids: Baker, 1991), 87.

17. For additional data on the original text of the Old Testament (other than the works already cited), see E.S. Kalland, "Establishing the Hebrew and Aramaic Text," in *The Making of the NIV*, 43–50; E.R. Brotzman, *Old Testament Textual Criticism: A Practical Introduction* (Grand Rapids: Baker, 1994); F.E. Deist, *Witnesses to the Old Testament: Introducing Old Testament Textual Criticism* (Pretoria: NGKB, 1988); C.E. Armerding, *The Old Testament and Criticism* (Grand Rapids: Eerdmans, 1983), 97–127; B.K. Waltke, "The Reliability of the Old Testament Text: Textual Criticism of the Old Testament and Its Relation to Exegesis and Theology," in *NIDOTTE*, ed. W.A. VanGemeren (Grand Rapids: Zondervan, 1997), 1:51–67; E. Tov, *Textual Criticism of the Hebrew Bible* (Minneapolis: Fortress, 1992); as well as the bibliographies and footnote references in all these resources.

18. J.R. Kohlenberger III, *Words about the Word* (Grand Rapids: Zondervan, 1987), 42.

19. P.W. Comfort, *Early Manuscripts and Modern Translations of the New Testament* (Wheaton: Tyndale, 1990), 16.

20. D.A. Black, *New Testament Textual Criticism: A Concise Guide* (Grand Rapids: Baker, 1994), 33.

21. B.M. Metzger, *The Text of the New Testament*, 3d ed. (New York: Oxford, 1992), 135.

22. Black, *New Testament Textual Criticism*, 63, 65.

23. R.H. Stein, *Luke*, NAC (Nashville: Broadman, 1992), 261 n. 216.

24. D.W. Burdick, "At the Translator's Table," *The [Cincinnati Christian] Seminary Review* 21 (March 1975): 19.

25. Comfort, *Early Manuscripts*, 213.

26. Ibid., 92.

27. J.H. Greenlee, *Introduction to New Testament Textual Criticism* (Peabody, Mass.: Hendrickson, 1995), 122. His entire discussion (pp. 122–23) is helpful. For "one and only" instead of "only begotten," see R.N. Longenecker, "The One and Only Son," in *The Making of the NIV*, 117–24, 163–64.

28. G.A. Riplinger, *New Age Bible Versions* (Munroe Falls, Ohio: A.V. Publications, 1993), 22.

29. For a more detailed treatment of this textual problem in Mark 10:21, see J.R. White, *The King James Only Controversy* (Minneapolis: Bethany House, 1995), 159–62.

30. For a fuller presentation see K.L. Barker, *The Accuracy of the NIV*, 16, 51.

31. S.L. Johnson, "Appendix 3: The Best Greek Text of the New Testament," in *The Accuracy of the NIV*, 109–10.

32. D.B. Wallace, "Inspiration, Preservation, and New Testament Textual Criticism," *GTJ* 12 (Spring 1991): 21–50.

33. J.W. Burgon, *The Revision Revised* (Collingswood, N.J.: Dean Burgon Society Press, repr. of 1883 ed.), 21 n. 2. Incidentally, Burgon's use of quotations from the early church fathers has been shown to have serious flaws and to lack in objectivity and accuracy. So his use of these sources is too unreliable to provide evidence for an early date of the Byzantine text-type. See M. H. Heuer, "An Evaluation of John W. Burgon's Use of Patristic Evidence," *JETS* 38 (December 1995): 519–30.

34. D.A. Carson, *The King James Version Debate* (Grand Rapids: Baker, 1979), 64; for a list of NIV New Testament passages that either explicitly state or strongly imply Christ's deity, see the *NIVSB*, Rom. 9:5n.; see also Barker, *The Accuracy of the NIV*, 66, 70–72.

35. See Z.C. Hodges and A.L. Farstad, eds., *The Greek New Testament According to the Majority Text* (Nashville: Nelson, 1982, rev. 1985), but see the review of this work by G.D. Fee in *TJ* 4 (1983): 107–13; see also W.G. Pierpont and M.A. Robinson, *The New Testament in the Original Greek according to the Byzantine/Majority Textform* (Atlanta: Original Word, 1991).

36. D.B. Wallace, "Some Second Thoughts on the Majority Text," *Bib. Sac.* 146 (July–September 1989): 276.

37. D.B. Wallace, "The Majority-Text Theory: History, Methods and Critique," *JETS* 37 (June 1994): 206.

38. Ibid., 209.

39. W.N. Pickering, *The Identity of the New Testament Text* (Nashville: Nelson, 1977).

40. D.A. Carson, *The King James Version Debate*, 105–23; D.B. Wallace, "The Majority Text and the Original Text: Are They Identical?" *Bib. Sac.* 148

(April–June 1991): 151–69; G.D. Fee, "A Critique of W.N. Pickering's *The Identity of the New Testament Text*: A Review Article," *WTJ* 41 (1978–79): 397–423.

41. H.A. Sturz, *The Byzantine Text-Type and New Testament Textual Criticism* (Nashville: Nelson, 1984).

42. B.M. Metzger, *The Text of the New Testament*, 293.

43. J.R. Kohlenberger III, *Words about the Word*, 47.

44. J.P. Lewis, *The English Bible from KJV to NIV* (Grand Rapids: Baker, n.d. [2d ed.]), 333.

45. Ibid., 334–35.

46. For numerous additional examples of a reasoned eclectic approach at work, see K.L. Barker, *The Accuracy of the NIV*, 52–102; J.T. Barrera, *The Jewish Bible and the Christian Bible*, 413–14; B.M. Metzger, *The Text of the New Testament*, 221–46; D. Ewert, *From Ancient Tablets to Modern Translations* (Grand Rapids: Zondervan, 1983), 160–62.

47. NKJV, Wide Margin Ed. (Nashville: Nelson, 1983), iv–v.

48. For additional data on the original text of the New Testament, see (other than the works already cited) R. Earle, "Establishing the Greek Text," in *The Making of the NIV*, 51–55, noting the works in the "Suggested Reading" list (55); G.D. Fee, "The Textual Criticism of the New Testament," in *Biblical Criticism: Historical, Literary and Textual*, 125–55; Fee, "Modern Textual Criticism and the Revival of the *Textus Receptus*," *JETS* 21 (March 1978): 19–33, plus the next three issues of *JETS* (all in 1978) for interaction between Fee and Z.C. Hodges; E.J. Epp and G.D. Fee, eds., *New Testament Textual Criticism: Its Significance for Exegesis* (Oxford: Clarendon, 1981); Epp and Fee, eds., *Studies in the Theory and Method of New Testament Textual Criticism* (Grand Rapids: Eerdmans, 1993); B.M. Metzger, *A Textual Commentary on the Greek New Testament* (Stuttgart: UBS, 1994); K. and B. Aland, *The Text of the New Testament*, trans. E.F. Rhodes (Grand Rapids: Eerdmans, 1987); P.W. Comfort, *The Quest for the Original Text of the New Testament* (Grand Rapids: Baker, 1992); M.W. Holmes, "New Testament Textual Criticism," in *Introducing New Testament Interpretation*, ed. S. McKnight (Grand Rapids: Baker, 1989), 53–74; H.A. Kent, Jr., "The King James Only?" *Spire* 12 (Fall 1983): 3–4, 11–12; D.K. Kutilek, "Erasmus: His Greek Text and His Theology," Research Report No. 32 (Hatfield, Pa.: Interdisciplinary Biblical Research Institute, 1986); B. Sheehan, *Which Version Now?* (Sussex, England: Carey Publications, n.d.); W.W. Combs, "Erasmus and the *Textus Receptus*," *Detroit Baptist Seminary Journal* 1 (1996): 35–53.

Chapter 4: *A Balanced Translation Philosophy*

1. M. Silva, *God, Language, and Scripture* (Grand Rapids: Zondervan, 1990), 134.

2. D. Taylor, "Confessions of a Bible Translator," *Books & Culture* (November–December 1995): 17.

3. M. Silva, *God, Language, and Scripture*, 134.

4. E.A. Speiser, *Genesis*, AB (Garden City, N.Y.: Doubleday, 1964), lxiii–lxiv.

5. Ibid., lxvi; see also H.M. Wolf, "Literal vs. Accurate," in *The Making of the NIV*, ed. K.L. Barker (Grand Rapids: Baker 1991), 125–34, 165.

6. E.A. Nida, *Toward a Science of Translating* (Leiden: E.J. Brill, 1964), 159–60.

7. E.L. Greenstein, "Theories of Modern Bible Translation," *Prooftexts* 3 (1983): 9–39; quoted by J.T. Barrera, *The Jewish Bible and the Christian Bible*, 126.

8. R. Elliott, "Bible Translation," in *The Origin of the Bible*, ed. P.W. Comfort (Wheaton: Tyndale, 1992), 233.

9. See C. Hargreaves, *A Translator's Freedom* (Sheffield: JSOT Press, 1993).

10. Several of these examples were given to me about 1990 by Dr. Marten Woudstra (now deceased), former professor of Old Testament at Calvin Theological Seminary.

11. M.E. Elliott, *The Language of the King James Bible: A Glossary Explaining Its Words and Expressions* (Garden City, N.Y.: Doubleday, 1967); see also E.H. Palmer, "The KJV and the NIV," in *The Making of the NIV*, ed. K.L. Barker (Grand Rapids: Baker, 1991), 140–54, 165.

12. R. Youngblood, "The New International Version was published in 1978—this is the story of why, and how," *The Standard* (November 1988): 18. For an example of such a "grotesque" rendering, see Bob Sheehan, *Which Version Now?* (Sussex, England: Carey, n.d.), 19.

13. *The Story of the New International Version* (Colorado Springs, Colo.: International Bible Society, 1978), 13 (italics mine).

14. K.L. Barker, "An Insider Talks about the NIV," *Kindred Spirit* (Fall 1978): 7.

15. S.M. Sheeley and R.N. Nash, Jr., *The Bible in English Translation* (Nashville: Abingdon, 1997), 44.

16. Ibid., 46.

17. *Report to General Synod Abbotsford 1995* from the Committee on Bible Translations appointed by Synod Lincoln 1992 of the Canadian Reformed Churches, 16.

18. Ibid., 42–63.

19. Ibid., 16.

20. Ibid., 169.

21. Ibid., 63.

22. *Acts of General Synod*, 122.

23. T. White, "The Best Bible Version for Our Generation," *The Standard* (November 1988): 12–14.

24. C.D. Linton, "The Importance of Literary Style," in *The Making of the NIV*, ed. K.L. Barker (Grand Rapids: Baker, 1991), 30.

25. E.A. Nida and C.R. Taber, *The Theory and Practice of Translation* (Leiden: E.J. Brill, 1982), 2.

26. Quoted in *A Bible for Today and Tomorrow* (London: Hodder & Stoughton, 1989), 19.

27. Quoted in *Reader's Digest* (September 1977): 95.

28. J. Callow and J. Beekman, *Translating the Word of God* (Grand Rapids: Zondervan, 1974), 23–24.

29. Thomas's chart essentially agrees with mine on the positioning of the NIV. See R.L. Thomas, "Bible Translations and Expository Preaching," in *Rediscovering Expository Preaching* by J. MacArthur, Jr., et al. (Dallas: Word, 1992), 311.

Chapter 5: *A Balanced Solution to Difficulties*

1. J.P. Lewis, *The English Bible from KJV to NIV* (Grand Rapids: Baker, n.d., 2d ed.), 67.

2. G. von Rad, *Genesis: A Commentary*, trans. J.H. Marks, OTL (London: SCM, 1963), 119.

3. See *NIVSB*, Matt. 1:17n.

4. See, e.g., E.A. Speiser, *Genesis*, AB (Garden City, N.Y.: Doubleday, 1964), 264–65; G.J. Wenham, *Genesis 16–50*, WBC (Dallas: Word, 1994), 312.

5. See also G.J. Wenham, *Genesis 16–50*, 384; E.A. Speiser, *Genesis*, 306–7; V.P. Hamilton, *The Book of Genesis Chapters 18–50*, NICOT (Grand Rapids: Eerdmans, 1995), 483.

6. *NIVSB*, Gen. 49:10n.

7. BDB, 1010; *šellōh* means lit. "which [referring back to 'scepter' and/or 'staff'] to him is" (= "which is to him" = "whose it is" = "to whom it belongs").

8. W.L. Moran, "Gen 49,10 and Its Use in Ez 21,32," *Bib* 39 (1958): 409–10 (following Dillmann and Sellin).

9. G.L. Archer, Jr., *A Survey of Old Testament Introduction* (Chicago: Moody, 1974), 482, 490.

10. K.L. Barker, *The Accuracy of the NIV*, 26–27.

11. See H.M. Wolf, "Literal vs. Accurate," in *The Making of the NIV*, ed. K.L. Barker (Grand Rapids: Baker 1991), 125–34, 165; cf. other figurative uses of "uncircumcised" in Lev. 19:23 ("forbidden"); Jer. 6:10 ("closed").

12. *NIVSB*, Lev. 3:1n.

13. K.L. Barker, *Micah* in *Micah-Zephaniah* by Barker and W. Bailey, NAC (Nashville: Broadman & Holman, 1999), 94; for a full discussion see N. Lohfink, *"ḥāram; ḥērem,"* in *TDOT* 5:180–99; for the alleged ethical problem of such "destruction" or "devoting to God," see P. Fairbairn, *The Typology of Scripture*, 2 vols. in 1 (Grand Rapids: Zondervan, n.d.), 2:406–15 (when considering this so-called problem, one must also remember that it was the Lord himself who later commanded the destruction of the pagan, idolatrous Canaanites—with their degenerate polytheism, sexual immorality, religious prostitution, and child sacrifice—in Deut. 7:2; 13:15; 20:17; Josh. 6:17; 10:40; 11:12, 20).

14. *NIVSB*, Exod. 25:17n.

15. Ibid., Lev 16:2n.; 17:11n.; for one of the better treatments of the Hebrew word used here *(kappōret)*, see R.E. Averbeck's article on the root *kpr* in *NIDOTTE* 2: 689–710; see also J.E. Hartley's "Excursus: *kpr*, 'make expiation, atone'" in *Leviticus*, WBC (Dallas: Word, 1992), 63–66.

16. K.L. Barker, *Micah*, 49–50; cf. N.H. Snaith, *The Distinctive Ideas of the Old Testament* (New York: Schocken, 1964), 24–32, 42–50.

17. K.L. Barker, "Grove," in *ZPEB* 2:851.

18. *NIVSB*, Num. 5:21n.

19. Ibid., Ezek. 47:15n.

20. A.R. Millard, "King Og's Iron Bed—Fact or Fancy?" *BR* 6 (April 1990): 20.

21. E.H. Merrill, *Deuteronomy*, NAC (Nashville: Broadman & Holman, 1994), 163.

22. E.S. Kalland, "Deuteronomy," in *EBC*, 12 vols., ed. F.E. Gaebelein (Grand Rapids: Zondervan, 1992), 3:64.

23. E.H. Merrill, *Deuteronomy*, 313.

24. R. Schultz, *"[špṭ],"* in *NIDOTTE* 4:213.

25. R. F. Youngblood, "1, 2 Samuel," in *EBC*, 3:591; see further E.S. Kalland, "Establishing the Hebrew and Aramaic Text," in *The Making of the NIV*, 48.

26. *NIVSB*, 1 Kings 19:3n.

27. G.H. Jones, *1 and 2 Kings*, 2 vols., NCBC (Grand Rapids: Eerdmans, 1984), 2:395.

28. *NIVSB*, 2 Kings 8:10n.

29. Ibid., 2 Chron. 26:21n.

30. M.E. Tate, *Psalms 51–100*, WBC (Dallas: Word, 1990), 510.

31. R.B. Dillard, *2 Chronicles*, WBC (Waco, Tex.: Word, 1987), 152.

32. D. Kidner, *Psalms 1–72*, TOTC (Downers Grove, Ill.: InterVarsity, 1973), 125–26.

33. J.A. Thompson, *1, 2 Chronicles*, NAC (Nashville: Broadman & Holman, 1994), 141, 295.

34. M.J. Selman, *2 Chronicles*, TOTC (Downers Grove, Ill.: InterVarsity, 1994), 415.

35. J.A. Thompson, *1, 2 Chronicles*, 288.

36. R.B. Dillard, *2 Chronicles*, 144.

37. *NIVSB*, Job 7:20n.

38. K.L. Barker, "The Value of Ugaritic for Old Testament Studies," *Bib. Sac.* 133 (April–June 1976): 122 n. 8.

39. *NIVSB*, Ps. 68:4n.

40. D.A. Garrett, *Proverbs, Ecclesiastes, Song of Songs*, NAC (Nashville: Broadman & Holman, 1993), 188.

41. *NIVSB*, SS 8:6n.

42. S.C. Glickman, *A Song for Lovers* (Downers Grove, Ill.: InterVarsity, 1976), 150.

43. *HALOT*, 1:7; see also R.E. Hayden in *NIDOTTE*, 1:248.

44. K.L. Barker, "The Value of Ugaritic for OT Studies," 127.

45. *NIVSB*, Jer. 25:26n.

46. Ibid., Jer. 51:1n.

47. Ibid., Ezra 5:12n.

48. Ibid., Job 1:17n.

49. D.J. Wiseman, "Some Historical Problems in the Book of Daniel," in *Notes on Some Problems in the Book of Daniel*, D.J. Wiseman et al. (London: Tyndale, 1965), 9–16.

50. T.J. Finley, *Joel, Amos, Obadiah*, WEC (Chicago: Moody, 1990), 139; similarly T.E. McComiskey, "Amos, Micah," in *EBC*, 7:282–83.

51. T.J. Finley, *Joel, Amos, Obadiah*, 211.

52. K.L. Barker, *The Accuracy of the NIV*, 49–50.

53. K.L. Barker, *Micah*, 96–98.

54. J.B. Lightfoot, *The Epistle of St. Paul to the Galatians* (Grand Rapids: Zondervan, 1957 [2d repr. ed.]), 154–55 (his excellent discussion of the Hebrew, Greek, Latin, and English words for "faith" and "faithfulness" continues on through p. 158); similarly C.F. Keil, *The Twelve Minor Prophets*, 2 vols. (Grand Rapids: Eerdmans, 1949), 2:71–74; D. Garland, "Habakkuk," in *Broadman Bible Commentary*, ed. C.J. Allen, 12 vols. (Nashville: Broadman, 1972), 7:258; R.D. Patterson, *Nahum, Habakkuk, Zephaniah*, WEC (Chicago: Moody, 1991), 211–23; D.J. Moo, *The Epistle to the Romans*, NICNT (Grand Rapids: Eerdmans, 1996), 75–79.

55. K.L. Barker, "Zechariah," in *EBC*, 7:683. This interpretation is supported, among others, by M.F. Unger, *Zechariah* (Grand Rapids: Zondervan, 1963), 214–15; H.C. Leupold, *Exposition of Zechariah* (Grand Rapids: Baker, 1965), 236–37; C.L. Feinberg, *God Remembers* (New York: American Board of Missions to the Jews, 1965), 229; H. Heater, Jr., *Zechariah* (Grand Rapids: Zondervan, 1987), 104; E.B. Pusey, *The Minor Prophets: A Commentary*, 2 vols. (Grand Rapids: Baker, 1950), 2:437–38.

56. K.L. Barker, "Zechariah," 683.

57. *NIVSB*, Matt. 5:22n.

58. Ibid., Mark 2:15n.

59. E.M. Yamauchi, "Did We Hear the Angels Right?" *CT* (May 16, 1994): 11.

60. *NIVSB*, Luke 17:21n.

61. Ibid., 1 Cor. 6:12n.; 6:13n.; see also 10:23n.

62. GKC, 471–72 (149).

63. *NIVSB*, Heb. 7:25n.

64. For his full discussion see R.L. Thomas, *Revelation 1–7: An Exegetical Commentary* (Chicago: Moody, 1992), 116–19.

65. For additional illustrations of CBT's balanced approach to solving problems, see K.L. Barker, *The Accuracy of the NIV*, particularly 19–50 (containing many examples of using Hebrew grammar, syntax, lexical studies, exegesis, theology, textual criticism, etc., in solving translation problems), as well as K.L. Barker, ed., *The Making of the NIV*.

Chapter 7: *Balance Is the Key*

1. W.T. Purkiser, "The Bible: Translation & Paraphrase" (Kansas City: Christian Service Training, Church of the Nazarene, n.d.), 5.

2. D.W. Burdick, "At the Translator's Table," 44.

3. D. Ewert, *From Ancient Tablets to Modern Translations* (Grand Rapids: Zondervan, 1983), 248.

4. D. Kucharsky, "The Latest Word," *Christian Herald* (November 1978): 32.

5. K.L. Barker, *The Accuracy of the NIV*, 103.

6. J.P. Lewis, *The English Bible From KJV to NIV*, 409–10.

7. M. Silva, "Reflections on the NIV," *New Horizons* 16 (June 1995): 4–5.

8. G.D. Fee and D. Stuart, *How to Read the Bible for All Its Worth* (Grand Rapids: Zondervan, 1982), 42.

9. D.N. Bastian, "We Have Been Bible Samplers Long Enough," *CT* (October 8, 1982): 104.

10. B.M. Metzger, "Handing Down the Bible Through the Ages: The Role of Scribe and Translator," 170.

Appendix

1. D. Ewert, *From Ancient Tablets to Modern Translations*, 203.

2. L.R. Keylock, "Bible Translations: A Guide Through the Forest," *CT* (April 22, 1983): 15.

3. J. Bright, *Jeremiah*, AB (Garden City, N.Y.: Doubleday, 1978), cxix–cxx.

4. R.G. Gromacki, "Which Translation Is Really Inspired?" *Journal of Adult Training* (ETA) 3/1 (n.d.): 11–17; see also E.L. Hushbeck, Jr., "Which Bible Is the Word of God?" *Affirm* 1 (May–June 94): 10–12, 23.

Bibliography

Although I have read and/or consulted numerous works in preparation for writing this one, I have included here only those actually quoted or referred to in this book. All abbreviations are spelled out in the list of abbreviations.

Acts of General Synod Abbotsford 1995 of the Canadian Reformed Churches.

Aland, K. and B. *The Text of the New Testament*. E.F. Rhodes, trans. Grand Rapids: Eerdmans, 1987.

Albright, W.F. "A New Hebrew Word for 'Glaze' in Proverbs 26:23." *BASOR* 98 (April 1945): 24–25.

Alden, R.L. *Proverbs*. Grand Rapids: Baker, 1983.

Allen, C.J., ed. *Broadman Bible Commentary*. 12 vols. Nashville: Broadman, 1972.

Archer, G.L., Jr. *A Survey of Old Testament Introduction*. Chicago: Moody, 1974.

Armerding, C.E. *The Old Testament and Criticism*. Grand Rapids: Eerdmans, 1983.

Averbeck, R.E. "[*kpr*]." *NIDOTTE*. 5 vols. W.A. VanGemeren, gen. ed. Grand Rapids: Zondervan, 1997. 2:689–710.

Baldwin, J.G. *Haggai, Zechariah, Malachi*. TOTC. Downers Grove, Ill.: Inter-Varsity, 1972.

Barker, K.L. *The Accuracy of the NIV*. Grand Rapids: Baker, 1996.

———. "Grove." In *ZPEB*. 5 vols. M.C. Tenney, gen. ed. Grand Rapids: Zondervan, 1975. 2:851.

———. "Hearing God's Word Through a Good Translation." In *Reading and Hearing the Word*. A.C. Leder, ed. Grand Rapids: CRC Publications, 1998, 17–31.

———. "An Insider Talks about the NIV." *Kindred Spirit* (Fall 1978): 7–9.

———, ed. *The Making of the NIV*. Grand Rapids: Baker, 1991.

———. *Micah*. In *Micah, Nahum, Habakkuk, Zephaniah* by K.L. Barker and W. Bailey. NAC. Nashville: Broadman & Holman, 1999, 21–136.

———, gen. ed. *NIVSB*. Grand Rapids: Zondervan, 1995.

———. "The Value of Ugaritic for Old Testament Studies." *Bib. Sac.* 133 (April 1976): 119–29.

———. "Zechariah." In *EBC*. 12 vols. F.E. Gaebelein, gen. ed. Grand Rapids: Zondervan, 1985. 7:595–697.

Barrera, J.T. *The Jewish Bible and the Christian Bible*. W.G.E. Watson, trans. Grand Rapids: Eerdmans, 1998.

Bastian, D.N. "We Have Been Bible Samplers Long Enough." *CT* (October 8, 1982): 104.

A Bible for Today and Tomorrow. London: Hodder & Stoughton, 1989.

Black, D.A. *New Testament Textual Criticism: A Concise Guide*. Grand Rapids: Baker, 1994.

Botterweck, G.J., and H. Ringgren, eds. *TDOT*. Vols. 1–9. Grand Rapids: Eerdmans, 1977–98.

Bright, J. *Jeremiah*. AB. Garden City, N.Y.: Doubleday, 1965.

Brotzman, E.R. *Old Testament Textual Criticism: A Practical Introduction*. Grand Rapids: Baker, 1994.

Brown, F., S.R. Driver, and C.A. Briggs, eds. *A Hebrew and English Lexicon of the Old Testament*. Oxford: Clarendon, 1907 (corrected 1972).

Burdick, D.W. "At the Translator's Table." *The [Cincinnati Christian] Seminary Review* 21 (March 1975): 1–47.

Burgon, J.W. *The Revision Revised*. Collingswood, N.J.: Dean Burgon Society, n.d. (repr. of 1883 ed.).

Callow, J., and J. Beekman. *Translating the Word of God*. Grand Rapids: Zondervan, 1974.

Carson, D.A. *The King James Version Debate*. Grand Rapids: Baker, 1979.

Childs, B.S. *Introduction to the Old Testament as Scripture*. Philadelphia: Fortress, 1979.

Combs, W.W. "Erasmus and the *Textus Receptus*." *Detroit Baptist Seminary Journal* 1 (1996): 35–53.

Comfort, P.W. *Early Manuscripts and Modern Translations of the New Testament*. Wheaton: Tyndale, 1990.

———, ed. *The Origin of the Bible*. Wheaton: Tyndale, 1992.

———. *The Quest for the Original Text of the New Testament*. Grand Rapids: Baker, 1992.

Cross, F.M., Jr. "The Contribution of the Qumrân Discoveries to the Study of the Biblical Text." In *Qumran and the History of the Biblical Text*. F.M. Cross, Jr., and S. Talmon, eds. Cambridge: Harvard, 1975. 278–92.

Deist, F.E. *Witnesses to the Old Testament*. Pretoria: NGKB, 1988.

Dillard, R.B. *2 Chronicles*. WBC. Waco, Tex.: Word, 1987.

Earle, R. "Establishing the Greek Text." In *The Making of the NIV*. K.L. Barker, ed. Grand Rapids: Baker, 1991. 51–55.

Eichrodt, W. *Theology of the Old Testament*. 2 vols. J.A. Baker, trans. Philadelphia: Westminster, 1967.

Elliott, M.E. *The Language of the King James Bible: A Glossary Explaining Its Words and Expressions*. Garden City, N.Y.: Doubleday, 1967.

Elliott, R. "Bible Translation." In The *Origin of the Bible*. P.W. Comfort, ed. Wheaton: Tyndale, 1992. 233–60.

Epp, E.J., and G.D. Fee, eds. *New Testament Textual Criticism: Its Significance for Exegesis*. Oxford: Clarendon, 1981.

———, eds. *Studies in the Theory and Method of New Testament Textual Criticism*. Grand Rapids: Eerdmans, 1993.

Ewert, D. *From Ancient Tablets to Modern Translations*. Grand Rapids: Zondervan, 1983.

Fairbairn, P. *The Typology of Scripture*. Grand Rapids: Zondervan, n.d.

Fee, G.D. Book review of *The Greek New Testament According to the Majority Text*. Z.C. Hodges and A.L. Farstad. *TJ* 4 (Spring 1983): 107–13.

———. "A Critique of W.N. Pickering's *The Identity of the New Testament Text:* A Review Article." *WTJ* 41 (1978–79): 397–423.

———, and D. Stuart. *How to Read the Bible for All Its Worth*. Grand Rapids: Zondervan, 1982.

———. "Modern Textual Criticism and the Revival of the *Textus Receptus*." *JETS* 21 (March 1978): 19–33.

———. "The Textual Criticism of the New Testament." In *Biblical Criticism: Historical, Literary and Textual*. R.K. Harrison et al. Grand Rapids: Zondervan, 1978. 125–55.

Feinberg, C.L. *God Remembers*. New York: American Board of Missions to the Jews, 1965.

Finley, T.J. *Joel, Amos, Obadiah*. WEC. Chicago: Moody, 1990.

Gaebelein, F.E., gen. ed. *EBC*. 12 vols. Grand Rapids: Zondervan, 1979–92.

Garland, D. "Habakkuk." In *Broadman Bible Commentary*. 12 vols. C.J. Allen, ed. Nashville: Broadman, 1969–72. Vol. 7 (1972).

Garrett, D.A. *Proverbs, Ecclesiastes, Song of Songs*. NAC. Nashville: Broadman, 1993.

Ginsberg, H.L. "The North-Canaanite Myth of Anath and Aqhat, II." *BASOR* 98 (April 1945): 15–23.

———. "Ugaritic Studies and the Bible." *BA* 8 (May 1945): 41–58.

Glickman, S.C. *A Song for Lovers*. Downers Grove, Ill.: InterVarsity, 1976.

Goddard, B.L. *The NIV Story: The Inside Story of the New International Version*. New York: Vantage, 1989.

Gordon, C.H. *Ugaritic Textbook*. Rome: Pontifical Biblical Institute, 1965.

Greenlee, J.H. *Introduction to New Testament Textual Criticism.* Peabody, Mass.: Hendrickson, 1995.

Greenstein, E.L. "Theories of Modern Bible Translation." *Prooftexts* 3 (1983): 9–39.

Gromacki, R.G. "Which Translation Is Really Inspired?" *Journal of Adult Training* (ETA) 3/1 (n.d.): 11–17.

Hamilton, V.P. *The Book of Genesis Chapters 18–50.* NICOT. Grand Rapids: Eerdmans, 1995.

Hargreaves, C. *A Translator's Freedom.* Sheffield: JSOT Press, 1993.

Harrison, R.K., et al. *Biblical Criticism: Historical, Literary and Textual.* Grand Rapids: Zondervan, 1978.

Hartley, J.E. *Leviticus.* WBC. Dallas: Word, 1992.

Hayden, R.E. *"[ʾbl]." NIDOTTE.* 5 vols. W.A. VanGemeren, gen. ed. Grand Rapids: Zondervan, 1997. 1:248.

Heater, H., Jr. *Zechariah.* Grand Rapids: Zondervan, 1987.

Heuer, M.H. "An Evaluation of John W. Burgon's Use of Patristic Evidence." *JETS* 38 (December 1995): 519–30.

Hodges, Z.C., and A.L. Farstad, eds. *The Greek New Testament According to the Majority Text.* Nashville: Nelson, 1982 (rev. 1985).

Holmes, M.W. "New Testament Textual Criticism." In *Introducing New Testament Interpretation.* S. McKnight, ed. Grand Rapids: Baker, 1989.

Hubbard, D.A. *Joel and Amos.* TOTC. Downers Grove, Ill.: InterVarsity, 1989.

Hummel, H.D. "Enclitic *Mem* in Early Northwest Semitic, Especially Hebrew." *JBL* 76 (1957): 85–107.

Hushbeck, E.L., Jr. "Which Bible Is the Word of God?" *Affirm* 1 (May–June 94): 10–12, 23.

Johnson, S.L. "Appendix 3: The Best Greek Text of the New Testament." In *The Accuracy of the NIV.* K.L. Barker. Grand Rapids: Baker, 1996. 109–10.

Jones, G.H. *1 and 2 Kings.* 2 vols. NCBC. Grand Rapids: Eerdmans, 1984.

Kalland, E.S. "Deuteronomy." In *EBC.* 12 vols. F.E. Gaebelein, gen. ed. Grand Rapids: Zondervan, 1992. 3:1–235.

———. "Establishing the Hebrew and Aramaic Text." In *The Making of the NIV.* K.L. Barker, ed. Grand Rapids: Baker, 1991. 43–50.

Kautzsch, E., ed. *Gesenius' Hebrew Grammar.* A.E. Cowley, reviser. Oxford: Clarendon, 1910.

Keil, C.F. *The Twelve Minor Prophets.* 2 vols. Grand Rapids: Eerdmans, 1949.

Kent, H.A., Jr. "The King James Only?" *Spire* 12 (Fall 1983): 3–4, 11–12.

Keylock, L.R. "Bible Translations: A Guide Through the Forest." *CT* (April 22, 1983): 10–15.

Kidner, D. *Psalms 1–72.* TOTC. Downers Grove, Ill.: InterVarsity, 1973.

Kitchen, K.A. *Ancient Orient and Old Testament.* Chicago: InterVarsity, 1966.

Koehler, L., and W. Baumgartner. *HALOT*. Vols. 1–4. W. Baumgartner, J.J. Stamm, et al., revisers. M.E.J. Richardson, trans. and ed. Leiden: E.J. Brill, 1999.

Kohlenberger, J.R., III. *Words about the Word*. Grand Rapids: Zondervan, 1987.

Kucharsky, D. "The Latest Word." *Christian Herald* (November 1978): 31–32.

Kutilek, D.K. "Erasmus: His Greek Text and His Theology." Research Report No. 32. Hatfield, Pa.: Interdisciplinary Biblical Research Institute, 1986.

Leder, A.C., ed. *Reading and Hearing the Word: From Text to Sermon*. Grand Rapids: CRC Publications, 1998.

Leupold, H.C. *Exposition of Zechariah*. Grand Rapids: Baker, 1965.

Lewis, J.P. *The English Bible from KJV to NIV: A History and Evaluation*. 2d ed. Grand Rapids: Baker, n.d. (1st ed., 1982).

Lightfoot, J.B. *The Epistle of St. Paul to the Galatians*. Grand Rapids: Zondervan, 1957 (2d repr. ed.).

Linton, C.D. "The Importance of Literary Style." In *The Making of the NIV*. K.L. Barker, ed. Grand Rapids: Baker, 1991. 13–31, 155.

Lohfink, N. *"ḥāram; ḥērem." TDOT*. Vols. 1–9. G.J. Botterweck and H. Ringgren, eds. D.E. Green, trans. Grand Rapids: Eerdmans, 1986. 5:180–99.

Longenecker, R.N. "The One and Only Son." In *The Making of the NIV*. K.L. Barker, ed. Grand Rapids: Baker, 1991, 117–24, 163–64.

MacArthur, J., Jr., et al. *Rediscovering Expository Preaching*. Dallas: Word, 1992.

McComiskey, T.E. "Amos, Micah." In *EBC*. 12 vols. F.E. Gaebelein, gen. ed. Grand Rapids: Zondervan, 1985. 7:267–331, 393–445.

McKnight, S., ed. *Introducing New Testament Interpretation*. Grand Rapids: Baker, 1989.

Merrill, E.H. *Deuteronomy*. NAC. Nashville: Broadman & Holman, 1994.

Metzger, B.M. "Handing Down the Bible Through the Ages: The Role of Scribe and Translator." *RR* 43 (Spring 1990): 161–70.

———. *The Text of the New Testament*. 3d ed. New York: Oxford, 1992.

———. *A Textual Commentary on the Greek New Testament*. 2d ed. New York: UBS, 1994.

Millard, A.R. "King Og's Iron Bed—Fact or Fancy?" *BR* 6 (April 1990): 16–21, 44.

Moo, D.J. *The Epistle to the Romans*. NICNT. Grand Rapids: Eerdmans, 1996.

Moran, W.L. "Gen 49,10 and Its Use in Ez 21,32." *Bib* 39 (1958): 405–25.

Nida, E.A. *Toward a Science of Translating*. Leiden: E.J. Brill, 1964.

———, and C.R. Taber. *The Theory and Practice of Translation*. Leiden: E.J. Brill, 1982.

Palmer, E.H. "The KJV and the NIV." In *The Making of the NIV*. K.L. Barker, ed. Grand Rapids: Baker, 1991. 140–54, 165.

Patterson, R.D. *Nahum, Habakkuk, Zephaniah.* WEC. Chicago: Moody, 1991.

Pickering, W.N. *The Identity of the New Testament Text.* Nashville: Nelson, 1977.

Pierpont, W.G., and M.A. Robinson. *The New Testament in the Original Greek According to the Byzantine/Majority Textform.* Atlanta: Original Word, 1991.

Purkiser, W.T. "The Bible: Translation & Paraphrase." Kansas City: Christian Service Training (Church of the Nazarene), n.d.

Pusey, E.B. *The Minor Prophets: A Commentary.* 2 vols. Grand Rapids: Baker, 1950.

Rad, G. von. *Genesis: A Commentary.* OTL. J.H. Marks, trans. London: SCM, 1963.

Report to General Synod Abbotsford 1995 from the Committee on Bible Translations appointed by Synod Lincoln 1992 of the Canadian Reformed Churches.

Riplinger, G.A. *New Age Bible Versions.* Munroe Falls, Ohio: A.V. Publications, 1993.

Ross, A.P. "Proverbs." In *EBC.* 12 vols. F.E. Gaebelein, gen. ed. Grand Rapids: Zondervan, 1991. 5:881–1134.

Sanders, A. A true story quoted from the *Houston Chronicle* in *Reader's Digest* (September 1977): 95.

Schultz, R. *"[špt]."* In *NIDOTTE.* 5 Vols. W.A. VanGemeren, gen. ed. Grand Rapids: Zondervan, 1997. 4:213–20.

Selman, M.J. *2 Chronicles.* TOTC. Downers Grove, Ill.: InterVarsity, 1994.

Sheehan, B. "Criticisms of the NIV: A Review Article." *Reformation Today* 114 (March–April 1990): 15–19.

———. *Which Version Now?* Sussex, U.K.: Carey Publications, n.d.

Sheeley, S.M., and R.N. Nash, Jr. *The Bible in English Translation: An Essential Guide.* Nashville: Abingdon, 1997.

Silva, M. *God, Language, and Scripture.* Grand Rapids: Zondervan, 1990.

———. "Reflections on the NIV." *New Horizons* 16 (June 1995): 4–5.

Snaith, N.H. *The Distinctive Ideas of the Old Testament.* New York: Schocken, 1964.

Speiser, E.A. *Genesis.* AB. Garden City, N.Y.: Doubleday, 1964.

Stein, R.H. *Luke.* NAC. Nashville: Broadman, 1992.

"The Story of the New International Version." Colorado Springs, Colo.: International Bible Society, 1978.

Sturz, H.A. *The Byzantine Text-Type and New Testament Textual Criticism.* Nashville: Nelson, 1984.

The Sunday Post of Glasgow, Scotland (March 26, 1995): 38.

Tate, M.E. *Psalms 51–100.* WBC. Dallas: Word, 1990.

Taylor, D. "Confessions of a Bible Translator." *Books & Culture* (November–December 1995): 17–18.

Tenney, M.C., gen. ed. *ZPEB*. 5 vols. Grand Rapids: Zondervan, 1975.

Thomas, R.L. "Bible Translations and Expository Preaching." In *Rediscovering Expository Preaching*. J. MacArthur, Jr., et al. Dallas: Word, 1992. 303–20.

———. *Revelation 1–7: An Exegetical Commentary*. Chicago: Moody, 1992.

Thompson, J.A. *1, 2 Chronicles*. NAC. Nashville: Broadman & Holman, 1994.

Tov, E. *The Text-Critical Use of the Septuagint in Biblical Research*. Jerusalem: Simon, 1981.

———. *Textual Criticism of the Hebrew Bible*. Minneapolis: Fortress, 1992.

Unger, M.F. *Zechariah*. Grand Rapids: Zondervan, 1963.

VanGemeren, W.A., gen. ed. *NIDOTTE*. 5 vols. Grand Rapids: Zondervan, 1997.

Wallace, D.B. "Inspiration, Preservation, and New Testament Textual Criticism." *GTJ* 12 (Spring 1991): 21–50.

———. "The Majority Text and the Original Text: Are They Identical?" *Bib. Sac*. 148 (April–June 1991): 151–69.

———. "The Majority-Text Theory: History, Methods and Critique." *JETS* 37 (June 1994): 185–215. This article is a longer version of an essay that originally appeared in honor of Bruce M. Metzger in *The Text of the New Testament in Contemporary Research: Essays on the Status Quaestionis* (SD 46; ed. B. D. Ehrman and M. W. Holmes; Grand Rapids: Eerdmans, 1994), 297–320.

———. "Some Second Thoughts on the Majority Text." *Bib. Sac*. 146 (July–September 1989): 270–90.

Waltke, B.K. "The *New International Version* and Its Textual Principles in the Book of Psalms." *JETS* 32 (March 1989): 17–26.

———. "Psalms 2 and 4." In *The Making of the NIV*. K.L. Barker, ed. Grand Rapids: Baker, 1991. 86–92, 159.

———. "The Reliability of the Old Testament Text: Textual Criticism of the Old Testament and Its Relation to Exegesis and Theology." In *NIDOTTE*. 5 vols. W.A. VanGemeren, gen. ed. Grand Rapids: Zondervan, 1997. 1:51–67.

———. "The Textual Criticism of the Old Testament." In *Biblical Criticism: Historical, Literary and Textual*. R.K. Harrison et al. Grand Rapids: Zondervan, 1978. 45–82.

Wenham, G.J. *Genesis 16–50*. WBC. Dallas: Word, 1994.

White, J.R. *The King James Only Controversy: Can You Trust the Modern Translations?* Minneapolis: Bethany House, 1995.

White, T. "The Best Bible Version for Our Generation." *The Standard* (November 1988): 12–14.

Wiseman, D.J. "Some Historical Problems in the Book of Daniel." In *Notes on Some Problems in the Book of Daniel*. D.J. Wiseman et al. London: Tyndale, 1965. 9–16.

Wolf, H.M. "Literal vs. Accurate." In *The Making of the NIV*. K.L. Barker, ed. Grand Rapids: Baker, 1991. 125–34, 165.

Wurthwein, E. *The Text of the Old Testament*. E.F. Rhodes, trans. Grand Rapids: Eerdmans, 1979.

Yamauchi, E.M. "Did We Hear the Angels Right?" *CT* (May 16, 1994): 11.

Youngblood, R. "The New International Version was published in 1978—this is the story of why, and how." *The Standard* (November 1988): 15–19.

———. "1, 2 Samuel." In *EBC*. 12 vols. F.E. Gaebelein, gen. ed. Grand Rapids: Zondervan, 1992. 3:551–1104

Hebrew Index

Greek Index

Name Index

Subject Index

Scripture Index

Dr. Kenneth L. Barker (B.A., Northwestern College; Th.M., Dallas Theological Seminary; Ph.D., The Dropsie College for Hebrew and Cognate Learning) is an author and speaker living in Lewisville, Texas. In the past he has served as executive director of the NIV Translation Center, academic dean of Capital Bible Seminary, professor of Old Testament at three theological seminaries, and visiting professor at two others. He is also general editor of *The NIV Study Bible* and author of commentaries on the books of Micah and Zechariah. *The Balance of the NIV* is the third volume in a trilogy focusing on the NIV. The other titles, also published by Baker, are *The Making of the NIV* and *The Accuracy of the NIV*.